BY

Amalie Adler Ascher

All arrangements by the author

THE
COMPLETE
FLOWER
ARRANGER

Simon and Schuster : New York

ISBN 0-671-21666-X
ISBN 0-671-22774-2 pbk.
Library of Congress Catalog Card Number 73-17695
Designed by Irving Perkins
Manufactured in the United States of America

5   6   7   8   9   10

To my father, Charles Adler, Jr.,
for the will to write,
and to both
Alice Anderson Ellison, Editor,
The Women's Pages, *The Baltimore Evening Sun,*
and Harold A. Williams, Jr., Editor,
The Baltimore Sunday Sun,
for the opportunity

ACKNOWLEDGMENTS

A book of this scope (and a first one at that) could not have been written without assistance from others. Therefore, I am most grateful to all those who have so generously helped me. Helen Van Pelt Wilson, my editor, heads the list both in importance and effort. Widely recognized as an author in her own right, she is a master of style and an expert on content. Working with her has been an education in itself.

Nor can I praise too highly the outstanding work of my two principal photographers, William L. Klender and Duane Suter, both with the magic touch that distinguishes true artistry.

My thanks also go particularly to: Mary F. FitzPatrick for producing a color wheel that exceeded my hopes; Faber Birren for direction in achieving the colored light effects in color plate 31 and for permission to reproduce his color triangle; Mrs. Margaret R. Mecaslin for advice on the color chapter; Dr. Curtis Marshall for reducing the complexities of lighting to understandable terms; Selma H. Adler for proofreading the manuscript and for constant encouragement; Mrs. B. J. Fine, my aunt, for lending her lovely table appointments; Dr. Elmer Worthley for sharing his extensive horticultural knowledge; Mr. Sofu Teshigahara, Headmaster of the Sogetsu School, who, on tour in Germany found time to select from my arrangements the one best exemplifying his modern style; Mrs. Walter D. Bahn, my first teacher, whose lessons I still follow; and the National Council of State Garden Clubs, Inc., without whose training this book could certainly not have been written.

I am grateful to those who graciously consented to my use of published material and photographs: Philip S. Heisler, Managing Editor, and *The Baltimore Evening Sun* for permission to reprint my articles comprising Chapters 9 through 14, and including some photographs; Harold A. Williams, Jr., Editor, and *The Baltimore Sunday Sun* for pictures and quotations from my articles from *The Sun Magazine*; Joan Lee Faust, Garden Editor, and *The New York Times* for permitting me to quote from my article, "It Isn't Hard to Avant-Garde"; Warren S. Park, Jr., Director, Programming and Operations, and the Maryland Center for Public Broadcasting for the use of a transparency from my television series, "The Flower Show"; and Mr. Tom L. Freudenheim, Director, and The Baltimore Museum of Art for permission to photograph my arrangements in their six marvelous period rooms, and to Mrs. Mary Beale Munford for patiently assisting.

For the beautiful flowers used in many of the photographs, I am indebted mainly to Clarence E. Litchfield, who managed to provide exactly what I needed even when the material was not generally available (his firm requested anonymity); Kurt Bluemel, who supplied many of the outdoor plants that were never less than blue-ribbon caliber; also Fred C. Bauer, florist. And for freely sharing their gardens—Mrs. J. Cookman Boyd, Jr., Mrs. Joseph I. Coale, Jr., Mr. and Mrs. M. Austin Fine, Dr. and Mrs. Edward F. Lewison, Mr. and Mrs. Malcolm W. Lowenstein, Mrs. J. Edgar Miller, Mrs. Ola M. Warner, and Dr. Wilson Lyon Grubb—and Mrs. Charles Knight for supplying me with house plants.

My thanks also to Helen B. Krieg, who typed my manuscript with unbelievable speed and competence, and to Julia Pentz for kindness in assisting me whenever I called; to my husband, Eddie, and my daughter, Candy, who without too much complaining traded a wife and mother for a book; to my three sons, Tommy, Johnny, and Kenny, for their enthusiasm and criticism (always objective). And last, because they deserve special thanks, my father for help in all forms; Mrs. Alice A. Ellison, friend and champion; and Mrs. Toku M. Sugiyama, Executive Director, Sogetsu, U.S.A., a talented arranger and teacher who instructed me in Japanese floral art and whose counsel and support have been with me in all my undertakings.

CONTENTS

My Kingdom. *Lots of counter and storage space, a work bench, walls of pegboard for hanging weathered wood, and window shades in several colors to pull down as backgrounds for photographing arrangements answer a flower arranger's every need, as here in the author's basement studio. Builder—The Welsh Construction Remodeling Company.* [KLENDER]

AUTHOR'S FOREWORD

Pick up any magazine on home furnishings and you will notice that indoor settings are seldom pictured without flowers or plants. Somehow, a home doesn't seem complete unless greenery or a burst of bloom gives it life. Although many decorators feel arrangements should have a spontaneous look so as not to distract from an interior display, I think a floral design deserves a more important role. When a composition of plant materials is thoughtfully planned, it can integrate color schemes and also provide a transition between heights of furniture. If, further, it is correlated to the style and period of a room, an arrangement can become one of its most attractive focal points.

Beside its practical benefits, floral designing offers personal dividends. It imparts a useful skill, and also brings self-satisfaction, relaxation, even recognition. Approached as a pastime, pursued as a hobby, and finally studied as an art, flower arrangement for me has been the means of realizing a childhood ambition to write. By exploring the subject from all angles as student and performer, exhibitor and judge, housewife and professional, I have encountered most of the problems and enjoyed many of the rewards. In this sharing of my knowledge and experience, I hope others will find in flower arrangement the key to success and fulfillment. If I could, so can you.

AMALIE ADLER ASCHER

Baltimore, Maryland
January, 1973

1

DISCOVER DESIGN

I still remember the first arrangement I made. Having more nerve than sense, I entered a flower show, although I had never worked with plant materials before. I suppose the design will remain forever etched in my memory, though it could hardly be called a design since there was no orderly pattern. I have forgotten the theme I interpreted, but to remind me of the occasion I have kept the pair of Japanese rice bowls that were used as containers. They had held jumbled bouquets of yellow and white daises, some greenery, and phlox and alyssum from my mother's garden. Uncoordinated, unsuited in style to any purpose, or in size to its location, my creation, of course, won no award nor even merited a sympathetic comment from my friends. But I didn't care; I had had fun expressing myself through flowers so to me my work was beautiful.

In essence, this is what arranging is all about. It is fascinating to study differences in forms; to experiment with their interactions; to observe the effect of colors on each other; to discover the number of patterns that can be created with plant materials. In the process, you become increasingly aware of your surroundings, sensitive to aesthetic experiences, curious about relationships, perceptive of potential in form and color, and driven to give these new dimension.

Designing is a matter of sorting and selecting, of analyzing,

BASIC TO DESIGN. *A central axis, skeleton, strong direction of movement, one or more centers of interest, and enough transition for change to take place gradually are the basic requirements for traditional designs.* [SUTER]

adapting and changing, of combining and eliminating, of enlarging on problems already solved. Unlike other arts, which transform a shapeless medium like paint or clay into meaningful images, floral composition begins with natural forms that are themselves artistic entities. Thus it seeks as end-product not so much a change in the identity of materials as their enhancement through harmonious relationships and new ways of presentation. Excellence in arranging, therefore, depends on knowledge of design, ability to recognize and develop the potential of materials, and some degree of creativity.

Stimuli of Design

My father is an inventor, holding more than sixty patents. He designs signal systems for airplanes, automobiles, and railroads. Although his work is far removed from flower arranging, I asked him to analyze his creative processes, believing that what activates his inventive mechanism should apply to other kinds of designing. He says ideas come if he just sits in his chair smoking his pipe and meditating, and the reason they come is because he is alert to new concepts. He is conscious of styling, of shapes, in contact with developments in his field, quick to make comparisons and form associations, familiar with problems, aware of inadequacies. Most important of all, he is forever questioning—why hasn't this been done before?—and always searching for improvement.

Although an aspect of creativity is the mulling over of thoughts, of accepting and rejecting ideas, a fertile imagination helps. However, the crux of the matter is that design is also the result of experience. It is stimulated by your environment provided you notice what you see. Inspiration comes from contact with familiar forms, discovery of strange ones, as well as your fantasies of nonexistent forms. The act of seeing must be developed to the point where you not only observe but relate and expand the field of vision beyond obvious associations. Conditioning your mind to receive ideas requires sensitivity to details as well as to generalities, to similarities as well as to differences. The ability to translate what you conceive in your mind's eye into a concrete image through selection and coordination of materials constitutes the fundamental process of designing.

Materials of an Arrangement

Before you can respond to stimuli, you must be familiar with the kinds of materials that compose an arrangement; these will be the means of converting your idea into reality. Aside from modern and line arrangements (discussed in other chapters), the basic needs of the more massive traditional designs (sometimes called

Conventional) are a central axis, a skeleton, a strong direction of movement, one or more centers of interest, and enough transition for change to take place gradually rather than abruptly. Three types of plants perform these functions, therefore some from each group are needed for most designs.

1. ELONGATED

Known as releasing forms, since they carry the eye up and outward, elongated materials also establish movement and dimension; at the same time they develop structure, outline, and a central axis.

ELONGATED PLANTS. *Lines of eremurus underlie construction, establish movement and dimension and develop structure, outline, and a central axis.* [SUTER]

Since these forms underlie construction, they are linear in character. Elongated flowers and foliage include spike forms—gladiolus and snapdragons—branches of trees and shrubs, vines, and long, pointed leaves, as ti, sansevieria, and yucca.

2. ROUND

To join lines and check their movement, round or cone-shaped forms act as stopping points as well as centers of attraction. Flowers are usually grouped in twos or threes, depending on size, and placed at repeated intervals. Thus they pace and continue eye movement rather than scatter attention or rivet it to a bull's-eye. This results when small flowers are spotted individually or one or two large ones, different from the rest, are placed directly in front. Volumetric or globular flowers are acceptable in this second category of mate-

ROUND. *Apples and grapes act as stopping points as well as centers of attraction, and at the same time join lines.* [SUTER]

rials, as carnations, roses, chrysanthemums, also crested or trumpet shapes, as celosias and lilies, even leaves when made into rosettes, as is possible with ivy and galax.

3. FILLER OR TRANSITION

Although elongated and round forms are essential for almost all designs, unless a composition is stark, something more will be needed to give fullness. This does not mean packing in excess material as though you were stuffing a turkey, but using as filler materials of intermediate size or of small bushy growth as compared to that of the line and globe forms. Besides rounding out a design,

FILLER OR TRANSITION. *As filler, phlox closes gaps, adjusts sharp differences of forms, and softens demarcation between them.* [SUTER]

filler closes gaps, gradually adjusts sharp differences of forms, and softens demarcations. For example, with the different forms of snapdragons and roses, use heather or acacia, related in character to both, for transition. In addition to airy materials, filler can be buds or miniature varieties of standard blooms (of carnations or marigolds, for instance), feathery clusters, or spraylike foliage and flowers as yew, boxwood, plumed celosia, freesias, sweet peas, statice, and pompon chrysanthemums.

The network of lines and round forms in an arrangement can be compared to a park. Paths provide routes from one area to another, but benches offer temporary pause, yet encourage walking after a rest to a terminal point. Such a course stimulates exploration, study, perhaps even a return trip to observe things missed the first time. An arrangement with no planned pattern of eye movement, or a pattern that is too active, tires the viewer so that he withdraws his attention and thus rejects the design.

Suitability of Materials

Besides selecting combinations of the three basic materials so that they harmonize with their surroundings, consider their usefulness as building material. When you collect flowers and foliages, their appearance will influence your selection at first, but even if colors are compatible and shapes well related, you are in trouble if stems are not of proper structure. These may be too short and spindly to establish a framework and strong lines of movement. They may be too weak for a firm axis. There may be no elongated forms tall enough to give height. And without sufficient length, how will you vary levels and planes? When captivated by a beautiful bloom, cast a critical eye at the stem; unless this qualifies as construction material or the deficiency can be corrected by mechanics (see Chapter 4), reject it and look for another.

Once the requirements of design and the potential of materials are considered as a single problem, you begin to develop an "eye" for the forms and patterns best suited to the needs of different types of arrangements. Examining a maze of branches, you will seek those that cascade or twist, knowing that these can make arrangements almost by themselves, and when you buy from a florist, you will select stems with good curves as they are more likely to create an interesting design than stiff straight ones. If you are a gardener interested in arranging, you will refrain from tying and staking all your plants, allowing some to grow crooked. Some deformity, even natural freaks, can be a means of creativity.

The character of materials determines the character of a design. For example, branches that are heavy or massive, like those of magnolia or red pine, produce an effect different from dainty pussy willow or leucothoe. The upright growth of leatherleaf viburnum makes a stiffer design than the curving carlesii variety.

You will find arranging easier if the lines of flowers and foliage fit the planned pattern of design. Strictly speaking, there are only two kinds of lines—straight and curved. Consequently, there are basically two broad categories of design: those based on straight lines—verticals, horizontals and triangles; and those owing their origin to curves—round, oval, and serpentine patterns. In each case, stems and design shapes usually correspond. However, though this is the most sensible way to make an arrangement, it is not the only one.

Actually it is possible to use curved lines to structure a linear pattern like a triangle or to suggest a circular outline with straight ones. It depends on the angles of placement. The illusion of a circle can be created by radiating a series of straight, evenly spaced lines of the same length around a central point. Nevertheless, it would be practically impossible to form an angular composition with curving materials, or to manipulate those that were forked into an undulating silhouette. Though matching stems to patterns of design generally reduces difficulty, an experienced arranger can be more flexible, able to evaluate design potential and thus turn almost any promising material to advantage.

Seeing Design

Once you become aware of it, you will discover design everywhere. In an open doorway that captures and defines space; in the play of shadows under changing light; in a shoe suggesting a free-form pattern. Think of such outlines as design sources for an arrangement. The doorway and the space it delineates constitute an opening within a rectangular frame; they make a pattern that could be enlarged by combining several such oblong shapes in different dimensions and positions. To apply the idea, you could bend the rushlike equisetum or stalks of mullein or pussy willow into intersecting angles, accented with sections of bark and canna blossoms.

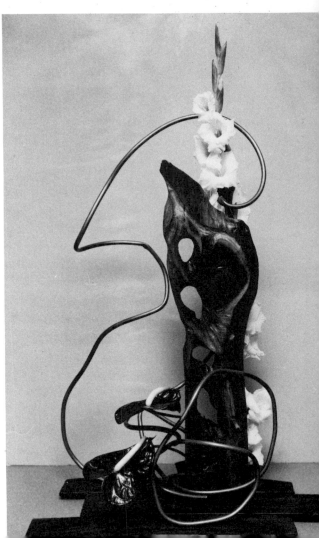

FROM SHOE TO ABSTRACT ART. *The oval of a shoe might suggest an unconventional pattern, and with copper tubing, driftwood, gladiolus, and anthuriums develop into an abstract design.* [HUTCHINS]

An innovative design would result and few would realize the inspiration was anything as simple as a doorway.

Shadows making irregular patterns in space might cause you to try overlapping large leaves of different shapes. As you mentally sort through familiar varieties, bird-of-paradise foliage, palm, and monstera come to mind, each of different outline. "Just right," you say to yourself, and you turn inspiration to reality by juxtaposing them in a container, one leaf slightly back of another.

You could interpret the oval of a shoe as interacting lines, solids, and voids and create an abstract design with copper tubing, anthurium, gladiolus, and a wood form, or develop a conventional pattern with loops of wisteria, anthurium, and hosta leaves. The significance of all of this is that a stimulus acts merely as a point of departure to set thoughts in motion. The inspiration is not to be reproduced as seen; rather, it serves as an idea for building something else.

In addition to noticing things as they are, look at the usual from a new point of view. For example, a triangle in normal position looks as steady and permanent as the Rock of Gibraltar. Now picture it inverted, balanced precariously on the tip. The uncertainty suggests a completely different design, but the same basic image has produced both concepts. Next, imagine other shapes you could build onto it, perhaps more triangles overlapping at various angles; perhaps a square and a rectangle intersecting; or a blockwork of lines behind the triangle and slightly to one side. One idea soon produces another.

The art of flower arrangement involves making a connection between the relationships of forms. Look at flowers and leaves as shapes, stems and branches as lines; experiment trying one against another to see which look best together. In any case, get involved. As you lose yourself in this absorbing study of patterns, colors, and textures, you will temporarily become oblivious to all else but the fun of designing.

BASIC DESIGN MATERIALS

For Line FLOWERS (GARDEN)

Astilbe	Iris
Bells-of-Ireland	Larkspur
Buddleia (Butterfly-bush)	Liatris
Canna	Lilac
Celosia	Lupine
Delphinium	Phlox
Foxglove	Physostegia
Forsythia	Snapdragon
Fruit Trees (Flowering)	Stock
Apple	Tritoma
Cherry	
Crab Apple	
Pear	
Plum	
Quince	

ROADSIDE

Cattails	Sea Oats
Dock	Sumac
Mullein	Thistle

VEGETABLES

Okra	Wheat

FOLIAGE

Aspidistra	Laurel
Azalea	Leucothoe
Beech	Magnolia
Bittersweet	Pine
Camellia	Podocarpus
Cedar	Sansevieria
Cotoneaster	Scotch Broom
Eucalyptus	Strelitzia (Bird-of-Paradise)
Fruit Trees (see Flowers)	Ti leaves
Gladiolus leaves	Viburnum
Grapevine	Willow (Corkscrew, Foxtail,
Grevillea	Pussy Willow)
Harry Lauder's Walking-Stick	Winged Euonymus
Iris leaves	Wisteria
Ivy	Yew
Juniper	Yucca

For Focal Areas

FLOWERS

Allium	Hydrangea
Anemone	Kale (Ornamental)
Anthurium	Lily
Aster	Marigold
Cabbage (Ornamental)	Peony
Cacti	Rose
Carnation	Stokesia
Celosia (Crested)	Strawflower
Daffodil	Strelitzia (Bird-of-Paradise)
Dahlia	Succulents
Daisy	Tulip
Geranium	Yarrow
Gerbera	Zinnia

FOLIAGE

Aucuba	Philodendron
Begonia (Rex)	Photinia
Ivy	Rhododendron
Monstera	Viburnum (Leatherleaf)

For Filler

FLOWERS

Acacia	Heather
Azalea	Lysimachia (Japanese Loosestrife)
Calendula	Lythrum (Purple Loosestrife)
Celosia	Queen-Anne's-Lace
Deutzia	Scarlet-Sage
Echinops	Spiraea
Everlasting	Statice
Feverfew	Sweet Pea
Fragrant Viburnum	Veronica
Freesia	Vitex
Gaillardia	

FOLIAGE

Andromeda	Laurel
Artemisia (Dusty Miller)	Ligustrum
Azalea	Pachysandra
Boxwood	Pittosporum
Fern	Santolina
Holly	Taxus (Yew)
Ivy	Thuja (Arborvitae)
Juniper	

ACCENT LEAVES

Aucuba	Croton
Begonia	Geranium
Bergenia	Hosta (Funkia)
Calladium	Ivy
Canna	Lotus
Castor Bean	Monstera
Coleus	Philodendron

2
ARRANGEMENT BY DESIGN

When you make an arrangement, you build a design. First you collect materials selectively, combining colors and textures that are harmonious, and then you work out a plan. It helps if you prepare for an arrangement as though you were assembling ingredients for a recipe. Keep in mind the approximate quantity of plant materials you will need as well as their apportionment of color and form; the number of spikes and round shapes; which shall be pale, which dark. Mentally organizing flowers and foliages as you select them makes arranging easier—for what you collect is just as important as how you put it together.

It doesn't matter whether you proceed spontaneously for pure enjoyment, imaginatively testing combinations and patterns as they occur to you (branches of red maple with pink tulips or red and white rubrum lilies for an oval mass); or if you deliberately devise a structure for a special purpose (perhaps a tall vertical for the piano in a blue and green living room). Your objectives will be the same —an harmonious and unified composition. This is rarely the result of chance.

Selection, then, is the first step; the second concerns composition. Flower arrangement, by definition of The National Council of State Garden Clubs, is the art of organizing the elements of design (comprising line, form, pattern, color, texture, and space) accord-

VISUAL MOVEMENT IN COUNTERBALANCE. *Line establishes proportion, balance, central axis, and direction—the structure of a design. To test balance, lay a string in a straight line through the center of the container from the tip of the branch to the base under the container. Material, in relatively equal amounts, arranged differently on each side of an imaginary vertical axis, illustrates asymmetric balance.* [SUTER]

ing to certain principles (including balance, contrast, dominance, rhythm, proportion, and scale). The elements are the qualities of matter that differentiate one thing from another. I find the elements easy to remember if I think of them in logical sequence. A work of art begins with a line that interacts with other lines to create a form. The form is distinguished by color and texture, and the whole makes a pattern in space.

The components of an arrangement are plant material, container, base, and accessories, the harmony of a design depending on their relationships as elements. They become unified if composed according to the principles, since these are responsible for visual stability (Balance), greater similarity than differences (Contrast), one prevailing characteristic (Dominance), continuous movement in a pronounced direction (Rhythm), and the proper size ratio of areas and parts (Proportion and Scale). Let us now examine each element and each principle.

ELEMENTS OF DESIGN

Line A line represents the visual movement between two points. In character it is curved, straight, or angular, continuous or broken, vertical or horizontal, weak or strong. Lines may radiate, crisscross, swerve in various directions, or wind around themselves.

The structure of a design begins with the placement of the first line of material. The position of this line creates the central axis: its length, the height; its angle, the direction of the design. If the primary line is upright, straight, and in the center, and other lines conform to it, the design becomes a vertical (as opposed to a horizontal or an S-curve).

A vertical design is basic but it can be made complex. By adding secondary lines at each side of the central line, size can be increased and shape altered to form a triangle. If two horizontal lines of the same length are placed on either side of the center line, and at equal distance from it, the base of a symmetrical triangle is formed. But, if one horizontal is one-third the length of the main line and inclines away from it at a 75-degree angle, and the other is half as long and set at 45 degrees, a different triangle results.

The triangle is developed with shorter auxiliary lines that follow and strengthen the three principal placements (center and two sides lines), and together they constitute the foundation. Design is completed by filling this in with other types of material. Generally, this is the procedure whereby lines structure an arrangement, a few basic ones forming the skeleton.

Line can be achieved in various ways, as by employing linear material—a curving branch, a loop of vine, a bladelike leaf, or a spike of florets; by placing stems in a vertical row; by using flowers in successive stages from bud to full bloom; or by graduating colors and sizes in sequence from the top, from light to dark, small to large, thin to thick. Line is related to rhythm since placements that compose lines also create rhythm.

Form   As with lines, forms also have character; they are delicate, graceful, massive, powerful, distorted, free-form, or geometric. A form may be completely solid or it may incorporate space if openings occur within its boundaries.

In floral art, the words form and shape are often used interchangeably, but they do have different meanings. A flat leaf is a shape; it has only a two-dimensional surface. A blossom is a form; it has depth. Many plant materials have strong linear qualities; they also have thickness that qualifies them as forms. Therefore, an arrangement is an assembly (but not an assemblage) of individual forms brought together for their compatibility and effect on each other.

Since flower arrangement is a three-dimensional art, like sculpture rather than painting, depth of form is an important factor in determining excellence. Depth depends on how plant materials are placed. If all are jammed together and occupy the same plane, the design will look flat, as though it were drawn on a sheet of paper. Such a fault can be corrected by varying the poses of materials, some flowers in profile, some in three-quarter view, and some, especially

FORMS HAVE CHARACTER. *Bird-of-paradise leaves, palm, and calla lilies are equally massive and powerful, yet forms are quite different, as is the shape of the wooden compote. (Compare size relationships and note that all agree in scale.)* [COPE]

those in the focal area, in frontal view. Other methods of achieving depth include placing shorter materials slightly behind taller ones in overlapping planes; graduating lengths of stems in the central area as they approach the rear thus gaining perspective as they recede; placing darker colors to the rear to draw the eye back in space; leaving space between stems; and, most important, finishing an arrangement at the back. If this is left bare, a design seems to fall away to nothing. But if sprigs of foliage or a few flowers are added at the back to cover exposed mechanics and stems, they round out the composition and complete it as well.

Pattern

Pattern applies to the contour of a composition and the grouping of materials within it. Pattern is monotonous if placements are uniform and forms unvaried, but it will be confused if assorted flowers are randomly spotted causing the eye to jump about. Although an arrangement may be composed of several different materials, a better design usually results if some are in groups of one kind. But a pattern may be visually tiring if forms, though similar in makeup and texture, nevertheless, make a busy pattern. For example, an arrangement composed only of shaggy materials—pine, chrysanthemums, plumed celosia, each a unit of multiple fine lines—would force the eye into excessive activity. Combining a small quantity of these fuzzy forms with a few of smooth texture, as roses or laurel foliage, would give the overall pattern needed relief.

Pattern relates to continuity, since the distribution of lines and forms can proceed either logically or in a disjointed way that disrupts unity. The pattern of a design and that of the individual materials influence each other. Consistency of character is desirable as curvilinear or angular rather than in a mixture, as would be the case if bird-of-paradise flowers were used in a serpentine design. The pattern within the body of the design should repeat that of the outline.

PATTERN AND SPACE. *A construction of dried laurel branches nailed together makes a linear pattern incorporating space to frame a tree-trunk container. Ti leaves and bird-of-paradise flowers contrast in form and color; dominating wood tones unify.* [COPE]

Patterns are of different kinds—intricate, bold, open, dense, regular, irregular. The pattern of the materials often identifies the style, as traditional, modern, oriental, or naturalistic.

Texture   Texture applies to tactile or surface qualities, the way something feels. Basically it involves the sense of touch, which is then experienced visually. For example, if velvet and steel wool are compared

NATURE'S VARIED TEXTURES. *The fuzzy-needled blue Atlas cedar is contrasted with the smooth, broad-leaved* Mahonia bealii. *The curved lines of the cedar establish a rhythmic pattern, the stiffer growth of the mahonia forms a center of interest.* [KLENDER]

mentally, their effect to the touch is imagined as well as their appearance.

In nature, texture helps to distinguish one plant from another, especially when foliage is similar in shape and shade of green. For example, the ground cover around my house is a combination of ivy and anchusa, but often unwanted violets must be weeded out. Since the leaves are similar, my garden helper had trouble determining which to pull, which to leave. When I pointed out the differences in feel, he could depend on his sense of touch rather than on sight.

The textural characteristics of an arrangement often set its tone, since material can vary from rough to smooth, coarse to fine, and shiny to dull. Texture can make a design formal or casual. Combined textures must be properly associated if the character of an arrangement is to be easily recognized. For example, the texture of an elegant porcelain container corresponds to the rich smooth texture of roses, lilies, and anemones; a pottery jug suits the simple ruggedness of marigolds and zinnias. The harmony of design is always affected by the relationship of textures.

Color Since Chapter 8 is devoted to color, it will only be mentioned here. Probably the most important factor in the compatibility of materials is their color, because color commands the most attention, causes the strongest reaction, and often accounts for success or failure. Understanding its influence and training your eye to make wise choices are essential to your success.

Space It is difficult to think of space as a positive element of design. Usually we regard it as emptiness without limits or definition. In a design, if we mark off space or enclose it, or if we cut out sections in a solid and leave them open, then space assumes shape. In a doughnut, a circular form encompasses a round opening that is part of the design; a lattice is a pattern of intersecting lines and square holes. If these examples are related to an arrangement, the significance of space *within* a composition becomes evident.

However, space must also be considered *around* a design when the surrounding area constitutes a frame, as a niche in a flower show or a chest in a hall. The designated space thus determines the dimensions and direction of an arrangement that must be made in relation to the outer area. Although space in this context has always controlled proportion, in the past it was not formally regarded as an element. The change in point of view has occurred as a result of the influence of modern art in which relationships between spaces and solids underlie most compositions. Space now heads the list of elements in flower arrangement; it must be taken into account in the first planning, and subsequently for its interaction with the forms of materials within the body of a design.

PRINCIPLES OF DESIGN

Balance   In addition to physical balance through firm mechanics, an arrangement must *look* steady. Indeed visual weight has more artistic significance than physical weight. Visual balance depends on two factors—alignment of the tip of the main stem with the center of the design, and apparent equal distribution of weight on each side of the vertical axis. Locating small forms, pale colors, and fine textures in the upper and outer regions of a design also prevents a top-heavy appearance. Paradoxically, an arrangement may be physically secure through good mechanics, yet lack visual balance.

In art, visual balance is usually equated with the human figure. In the normal position, the body is erect, the head centered directly above the arches of the feet. We say posture is good when it conforms to this standard.

The structure of a flower arrangement can be compared to the human figure. A tall, sturdy piece of plant material forms the backbone of the design, establishing a central axis. Its tip is the head and the angle of placement in relation to the center gives equilibrium to the composition. Auxiliary stems following the direction of the primary line reinforce it with visual support. Secondary materials at the sides give the arrangement form. Fillers in between strengthen the design. Good mechanics provide footing. The heart in the central area creates the focus.

If two children of the same weight straddle a seesaw, they will create perfect balance and suspend movement. However, a red and a pink carnation may weigh evenly on a scale, but when placed side by side to flank a vertical axis, they throw it out of balance because the darker hue looks heavier. The same visual imbalance occurs between coarse and fine textures, open and closed forms, large and small sizes. For example, a dahlia and a fuji chrysanthemum do not balance visually because the broad compact petals of the dahlia look heavier than the thin airy ones of the chrysanthemum. The coarse texture of yucca foliage gives it greater visual weight than the smooth leaves of lirope.

To balance a composition, forms of light visual weight are usually best placed higher in a design, and dark massive materials grouped lower to contribute weight at the base where it is needed. Equal distribution on each side of a central axis can be accomplished by matching like against like (symmetrical balance), or by increasing the number of weaker forms on one side to compensate for a fewer number that are visually heavier on the opposite side (asymmetrical balance).

Symmetrical and Asymmetrical Balance

In floral design, symmetrical and asymmetrical balance are also known as formal and informal balance. Symmetrical balance is usually produced by a triangular shape composed of identical materials in the same relative positions on each side of the central axis. One half mirrors the other half as though an imaginary line were drawn vertically through the middle. Symmetrical designs are associated

SYMMETRIC BALANCE. *In a long-lasting triangular design, leucothoe, fresh celosia, and plastic marigolds almost repeat each other in number and position on each side of the central axis.* [KLENDER]

ASYMMETRIC BALANCE. *In an arrangement that "wears and wears," green boxwood and variegated aucuba are used with fake yellow daisies and carnations, one half the design compensating for the other half in visual weight, though placements differ.* [KLENDER]

with formality and elegance and are attributed to earlier periods in art that are identified with the same formal characteristics.

Asymmetrical composition, shaped like the letter L or S, achieves balance through compensation. The amount of material on each side of the central line must appear comparable, even though types and numbers may not be identical. The combined weight on one side equals that on the other, the differences compensating visually. For example, if a red peony were used on the right side of a design, two white ones could probably balance it on the left.

Balance in a composition is similar to mathematics. Although seven and seven make fourteen, so do ten and four, and eight and six. In an arrangement, if the number of flowers and foliage is the same on each side of the central axis, usually their characteristics must be identical also. If the numbers are different, some quality of form, color, or texture must make up the deficit through visual weight to compensate for the imbalance.

Dominance and Contrast

Through dominance and contrast a design gains both unity and variety. Dominance comes with repetition; contrast, through change. Each depends on the other. For dominance, at least two different characteristics must be present, one subordinate to the other. When quantities are equal, nothing stands out and a composition divides in half or into sections. Repetition ensures continuity by providing one element that pervades a design, thus uniting it.

But if there is only sameness, a design lacks interest. Contrast provides change of pace. It may be extreme, as between angular and round forms, or subtle, as circles and ovals that deviate only slightly and therefore attract less notice. Gradual change depends on transition to integrate extreme differences in form or color. This is achieved by gradation in sizes, shades, or stages of development, as from bud to mature bloom. Contrast, like dominance, should be used in unequal amounts. Since it is a means of accent, contrast must be subordinate, not so excessive that it becomes dominant, yet of sufficient importance to be effective.

Contrast creates variety that stimulates interest; dominance through repetition provides a unifying factor of continuity. Therefore, in planning a design, let one color, one plant material, or one form predominate. To avoid monotony, relieve similarities by introducing a smaller quantity of differences.

Rhythm

It is rhythm that draws the eye through a design. Without rhythmic flow, a composition appears lifeless. Rhythm is created by patterns of materials that form orderly paths of eye travel from one area to another. As in music rhythm sets the mood of a design. Movement may be lively, strong, or sudden; it may be graceful, continuous, or unhurried. The greater the adjustments the eye must make to the activity of lines, to wide jumps in intervals, to abrupt changes in directions, the faster the movement and the sharper the excitement. The closer the spacing and the smaller the differences between sizes, forms, and shades, the easier the assimilation, the more leisurely movement will proceed and the more placid the effect.

Mood through rhythm also indicates the style of an arrangement. The greater the deviation of movement, the more modern the design; the more closely related the lines of travel, the more traditional the design.

Since rhythm depends on line, both are produced by the same means: linear plant material; repetition of color, form, or kind of material to make a visual path; or by gradation from one stage to the next. Rhythm may be forceful, a few lines moving in one direction, as is usually the case with simple compositions, or in more complex works, weaker lines added to take a different course from the established one, as when a diagonal line intersects a main vertical. Increasing the number of directions shifts attention and varies design, but departures should be kept to a minimum (modern design excepted), the secondary lines subordinated to the stronger central flow. For circular motion, radiating lines augment size and fullness, sending the eye to the outer edges of an arrangement, thereby creating visual gradations around the perimeter.

Although the term rhythm usually suggests grace, movement may also be twisted or angled. The easiest way to institute rhythm and also produce lively action is by line direction that utilizes the natural growth patterns of plants. Bare curving branches, crooked stalks, curled vines, or large individual leaves oddly bent are good means of rhythm. When two or more similar types are combined, they can often make an entire design, and this is called a line arrangement. It depends for emphasis on minimal amounts of other material that in excess would destroy the spacious freedom of line.

Proportion and Scale

Proportion and scale are so similar that they are often confused. Yet a distinction is made between them in flower arrangement. Proportion determines height and width of an arrangement in relation to space and container—how tall or short materials must be, how long and wide a base or mat underneath for all to fit comfortably together. If a design is too low for a vase or equal to it in height, the fault lies in proportioning. Proportion applies to the measurement of one part of a design to another, as well as to the dimensions of the display area. (There is more on proportion in Chapter 20, under Niches.)

Scale is a matter of size in the sense of how big or how small a flower, leaf, or accessory should be in relation to the size of the container, the arrangement, and the furniture on which it stands. Thus an iris and a violet would be out of scale, so different are they in size. A wine glass is too small a container for a piano; a butterfly the size of a grapefruit too large to rest on a leaf. However, though a bowl and the plant material might be small enough for a dainty French table, the floral design might be so massive that it sprawled over the edge. Then the scale would be correct since the size ratio between furniture, container, flowers, and foliage individually would be consistent, but the proportion would be wrong because the quantity of material and the measurements of the arrangement would exceed the display space. A thimble is another example. Compared to a dining table it looks minuscule. Place it in a doll-house and the thimble appears enormous. The change in size relationships has affected scale.

In determining proper scale between components of an arrangement, remember the Three Bears—not too big, not too small, but "just right." For proportion, not too much, not too little, but "just enough."

3

COLLECTING CONTAINERS

Once you become interested in flower arranging, you find yourself with another hobby—collecting containers. Even when your cupboards apparently hold containers of every imaginable color, shape, and size, you go on encountering others slightly different, each answering a present need or holding promise for the future. It seems easier to find reasons for acquiring just one more container than to resist a lucky find.

Still your approach to collecting should be practical. Each contemplated purchase should be evaluated to determine if, indeed, it will make a positive contribution. Otherwise you may amass a conglomeration of white elephants fit only for the school bazaar or rummage sale of your favorite charity. In fact, such events provide excellent examples of what *not* to buy. Rarely does a treasure turn up among the cast-offs, which are usually characterized by garish colors and decoration, too shiny finishes, grotesque shapes, outlandish sizes, and freakish proportions.

Worthless containers are often squatty, bulging in the wrong places, unbalanced on spindly legs or a shrunken base, or with necks too long and narrow to admit more than a few stems. Many repudiate the accepted precept, "form follows function." Instead of conforming in design to their task, they are molded into shapes unrelated to plant materials; they simulate animals or clothing, as shoes or hats or toys, telephones, or dad's pipe to name a few of the worst offenders. Rather than observing another dictum, "honor the integrity of materials," containers often pretend to be something they are not. Falsifying their origins, they become cheap imitations: plaster is finished to look like wood, marble, or alabaster; glass fakes precious metals or jewels; plastic masquerades as fine china. In these cases, the container is not true to itself either in design or materials.

Factors in Selection

In flower arrangement, container has connotations beyond the dictionary definition of "a thing that contains"; it encompasses more than vases and bowls, box, can, jar, or crate. In floral work, a container transcends its practical purpose and becomes an artistic component of design, an integral part of it.

Thus two factors—size and decorative qualities—determine the suitability of a container to a design. As the first requirement is to hold materials, it must have an opening adequate for a number of stems and a quantity of flowers and foliage as well as enough water to sustain them. Arrangement and container must be in proportion, the container neither so large that it overpowers the arrangement nor so small that the design dwarfs the vase. A container must be sturdy enough to balance the weight and breadth of a quantity of material.

Decoratively a container may be of little interest or it may make a positive contribution through color, form, or texture. Except in modern design where it may be featured, a container is usually of less importance than plant material. In any case, a container should share the characteristics of a design, be equally formal or casual, be related in color but not so intense or varied in hue, highly glazed or patterned that it competes. Compatibility also depends on similarity of style and shape, container and design correspondingly traditional, modern, naturalistic, or oriental. For example, a graceful, delicate vase would not be suitable for an imposing angular branch design. The color, texture, and style of a container should be in keeping with the setting or mood of an occasion, and have the same degree of elegance or informality, the same air of gaiety or restraint. Thus, a straw basket would not be right for a room of satinwood and damask; or a bronze Japanese urn for a golden wedding anniversary.

In collecting your containers, be guided also by the dimensions and shape of the area and furniture you will use for their display and for the type of arrangements you like to make. Decide if you need a tall, narrow design for one location in your home, a low horizontal for another. Do you require containers for large tree branches, for dainty miniatures, simple impromptu designs, or special events? Will your containers be used to brighten subdued surroundings or to blend with a colorful environment? If your interest is mainly in competition, collect containers that will be in proportion to properties used most frequently by your club. You might also need several sizes and shapes for different stagings as on a pedestal, in a niche, or on a dining table. Usually, especially for standard designs, a container that suits your home will also adapt to exhibition work.

Basic Containers   Although every household has receptacles from tin cans, cook- and tableware, to family heirlooms that can be converted to containers, some of these require considerable skill, while others are not decorative. If you are starting a collection, select a few standard shapes—a shallow bowl, cylinder, compote, goblet, and urn. Plain colors blend with most plant material, but the best hues for containers are shades of green, woody tones, mustard, beige, tan, or rust. However, if you are as partial to pink as I am, then add at least one container in a rosy tint to use for a traditional design of pastel flowers. (Neutrals are useful also; for guidelines on these, refer to Chapter 8 on color.) To begin with, avoid metal receptacles with high luster finishes, as copper and brass, for these are difficult to integrate and tend to dominate a design. Silver need not be avoided, as its surface is not excessively bright unless highly polished.

A Few for Many Needs. *Collection of versatile yet practical containers.* Top shelf: *Compotes in metal, glass and silver combined, and basketry.* Second shelf, left to right: *Low rectangular bowl, goblet, cylinder, low square bowl.* Third shelf, left to right: *Clay jug, metal pillar vase, flared pewter vase, wood bucket, lustreware urn.* Fourth shelf: *Modern ceramic pots stand beside and in front of a pottery vase.* [SUTER]

Fundamental for practice and very versatile are a flat shallow bowl and a ceramic cylinder in a solid color. Empty, neither is likely to win compliments and both are quite ordinary, but like the basic black dress adorned, each shows to advantage almost all plant material and can be used for a number of designs from vertical to circular, for line or mass, traditional or modern. Even experienced arrangers employ a low bowl or cylinder to whip up arrangements in a hurry or on days when inspiration refuses to come.

Easiest to use is a low bowl, round or rectangular, 7 by 14 inches or 10 to 12 inches in diameter, and 3 inches deep with straight sides, the opening the size and shape of the base. Such a container suits most compositions unless they extend over the rim in front in an S-curve or diagonal. For these you need a tall container and this is also appropriate for other designs. The standard 10 to 12 inches high cylinder is less difficult than other types of vases but the mechanics are one step above those for a low bowl. (See Chapter 4.) Should you wish to improvise rather than buy these containers, substitute a Pyrex pie plate or baking dish painted to harmonize with arrangements, or a large juice or coffee can for the cylinder, this painted or covered with adhesive-backed paper. If you need more height, solder two together, first removing both ends from the top can.

A cylinder and a shallow bowl in matching or complementary colors can be used together in a two-level design or combined to make a compote-type vessel, the bowl on top of the cylinder serving as pedestal. Such inventiveness was suggested by my first teacher who incorporated pieces of silver hollowware into elevated containers for formal centerpieces on her dinner table. She would set a candy dish on a candlestick or up-end a compote (the top becoming the base) to elevate a small vegetable dish or just its cover. Long-stemmed goblets, inverted under a glass dessert or finger bowl, a deep dish, or large ashtray give the same effect. As you put your imagination to work, you will probably think of other possibilities.

Compotes and Related Shapes

Once the cylinder and bowl have been mastered you are ready for a compote. Certainly the compote is my favorite container, especially for the dining table. Tall ones on a pedestal are the most graceful of all forms. However, just any compote won't do. Some antique types are cumbersome, the bowl too large, too shallow, or with a wide flange that makes it impossible to draw plant material over it to soften the rim. Short compotes often look squatty, so choose those that are well-proportioned. In my collection I have several styles of assorted wares—alabaster, basketry, ceramic, cut crystal, metal (brass, bronze, iron, ormolu, pewter, silver, and tin), plexiglass, and wood to suit traditional, modern, and oriental designs. Some have round openings, others oval. For general use, I prefer a compote with 6-inch opening, 9 to 14 inches high, and a 2- to 4-inch depth.

You can also improvise compotes, employing various props for a pedestal—a baluster, wooden blocks round or square, cardboard roller, a chair or table leg, a length of metal pipe, plastic tube, or rolling pin without handles. Fasten any one of these to a wood base made of half-inch unfinished plywood from a lumber yard. For the top, use a ceramic, glass, or plastic cereal bowl, a funnel, cup needle-holder, or a small shallow gilded tin bowl from the florist. Connect

LOOK FOR THE UNUSUAL. *A compote designed as a Greek temple is "different," has graceful proportions and a roomy interior.* [COPE]

parts with glue and reinforce seams with floral clay. Or pass through the center of a hollow pedestal a metal rod or bolt threaded at each end, first drilling holes in bowl and base for attaching each to the rod with a nut. Sink nut in base and seal with melted paraffin around the nut in the bowl to prevent leakage. Paint the compote a color or spray a wood tone, or antique it in a metal finish.

Tin cans stacked and glued together are also a source for compotes. You can choose from several combinations of heights and diameters; one of the best incorporates as a shaft a 12-ounce juice can fastened to an 8-ounce vegetable or sauce can. Two tuna cans (or cans for sliced pineapple or bamboo shoots) each make a top and a bottom. Since this improvised container is lightweight when empty, fill the two center cans with sand or Kitty Litter before gluing top and bottom. If you wish, a slightly larger lid can make a base. Although not glamourous, a compote of cans, painted or sprayed, serves a useful purpose and its humble origin is not apparent when it is filled with plant material. Tin-can compotes are always excellent for fund-raising projects, as they are cheap and easy to make and do not require large or costly arrangements.

Of similar shape are goblets and chalices. Department stores and gift shops carry oversized goblets, some opaque, some transparent. Either, beside conventional use as container, may be inverted and a deep plate or shallow bowl placed on top of the base of the stem to hold an arrangement. In this position, a large clear goblet can become a two-tiered design if a second plate with a cup needle-holder is placed under the upturned goblet to hold a few blossoms and sprigs of foliage. When different units are treated as one, they should match or share characteristics.

Vases

Some idea of the great variety of vases is seen in a rare manual (only two hundred copies) published by The Walpole Society in 1914. *The Ceramic Collectors' Glossary* by Edwin Atlee Barber describes forty different types, and these are just a few of the many

VASES, VASES, VASES. Left front. *Easiest to use is the trumpet-beaker.* Far right. *Most difficult is the jar with the neck set in the bulge of the swelling shoulders; the others all useful shapes.* [SUTER]

forms. Among these my favorite for easy arranging is a "Trumpet-Beaker," with a rim that spreads outward thus permitting the insertion of stems at varying angles without wiring or bending. An urn with similar opening also permits easy manipulation of stems. But since the body of an urn is more massive and formal than a slender beaker, the urn usually requires a more imposing design. However, when you choose urns, or for that matter any vessel with a handle,

STRICTLY JAPANESE. Left to right: *Boat, two styles of two-tiered containers,* usabata, compote, *and at* front-center, *a* sunabachi. [SUTER]

as a teapot or pitcher, avoid those with handles that reach above the mouth as these are likely to interfere with the arrangement.

For traditional Western compositions, a vase with a tapered neck and flared top is preferable to a jar with swelling shoulders extending beyond a small neck and mouth or a jar without a neck, the opening set directly in the bulge. Since these jars are often of Chinese origin, they are better suited to oriental than Western styles. One type that Barber's Glossary terms a Baluster was made especially for flowering branches; others include the "oviform—shaped like an egg on end, and the Pyreform—that looks like an inverted pear."

Jardinieres and Other Objects

A jardiniere or cachepot combines characteristics of vase and bowl being midway in height between tall and shallow containers and with a wide opening. Since these vessels were originally intended for potted plants rather than for arrangements, they are usually decorated with some painted motif. Thus a jardiniere or cachepot requires greater care in coordinating with floral designs, but this should not disqualify them since form and proportion are otherwise pleasing. Especially suitable are antiques or copies of Wedgwood, lovely with all-white mass compositions, and French styles in the Sèvres manner, the colors in harmony with delicate pastel flowers.

But once you begin collecting antiques, you have really lifted Pandora's lid. Your quest for the old will lead you to a wide selection of household wares, many manufactured in European factories no longer in existence. The long list includes: candy dishes, cigarette holders and ashtrays, baskets, bean pots, bottles, buckets, cornucopias, caudle cups and pots, decorative boxes, decanters, inkwells, jars, jugs, lamp bases, mortars, muffineers, mugs, pepper shakers, perfume bottles, pitchers, roll tops and vegetable dishes, salt boxes and salt cellars, sauce boats, scales, sugar bowls, tankards, tea caddies, tureens, and wine coolers. Avoid punch bowls or any pieces like them that are large, circular, and deep, as salad or kitchen mixing bowls; also avoid those with potbellies or with a broad, flat ring or lip around the rim. In my opinion, these head the list, along with clear glass receptacles and teapots and pitchers with attached lids, as the most difficult of all containers.

When you buy modern ceramics, beware of containers with tiny holes, tubular openings protruding at angles that make it difficult to balance flowers, and cavities too narrow from front to back to accommodate stems.

Candlesticks

No collection is complete without at least one candlestick, 12 to 18 inches tall. Candlesticks are among my favorites, lending grace to dining-table designs, casual or formal. Through the years, I have acquired a number in different styles and materials, some in pairs, others singly, always reassuring myself such purchases are practical. Important is stability, the base sturdy enough to support plant material at the top. (Mechanics for converting candlestick to container are described in Chapter 4.)

In advanced work, one or two candelabra may be used to support one arrangement or a pair. In this instance, the cups hold candles as was intended. To fasten flowers, a block of Oasis wrapped in green foil and chicken wire is wired to each arm of a two-branched style. One candelabra containing both flowers and candles may occupy the center of a dining table or two with corresponding designs placed one at each end. When a large candelabra with several lights is used alone, instead of attaching Oasis to the arms, two blocks are placed to flank the central shaft. Of course, in all such arrangements, the height of the flowers must be kept well below the top of the candles to avoid danger of fire.

Imaginative Containers

If you have a fertile imagination and are handy, you can adapt almost any object to your purpose even if it is unrelated to flower arrangement. Almost anything with a cavity can be considered if it is

DON'T TELL ME! *You guessed it—a car spring, fitted with a cupholder, makes a modern container for boxwood and anthurium.* [PEARSON]

OH, NO! OH, YES! *A sewer pipe wrapped with hardware cloth becomes a vase for a simple design of furled ti leaves and bunches of allium.* [PEARSON]

the right size, of interesting shape, well-proportioned, and of distinctive texture. The ingenuity of arrangers is amazing; you have only to attend flower shows to see multiple examples of improbable transformations. Lamp bases, bird cages, candle molds, car springs, electrical equipment, light fixtures, machinery, sewer pipes, and stove tops have all served as containers.

Then there are natural forms, some with ready-made openings, others hollowed out. These include wide strips of bark glued together, coconut shells, coral, driftwood, gourds, minerals, palm spathes, lava rock, logs, roots, and sea shells. Many arrangers consider these priceless, though free for the finding.

Make Your Own Though the world is full of containers, you may sometimes want to make your own. Tin cans can be disguised, not only with paint, but with shellac and a coating of crushed eggshells, perlite, or sand, with decorative bits of glass or stone, a wrapping of flexible bamboo or mirrored placemats, hardware cloth, or metallic air-conditioning filters. You can even wind a can with string.

If you can hammer a nail straight (I can't), containers may be fashioned from sections of molding, panels, or plywood, the four sides and a bottom fitted together. For feet, use empty spools or coat hooks.

Four-pound sheet lead from a plumbing-supply house may be cut to size and shape with tin snips. A frame, such as a baking loaf pan, placed in the center can serve as guide for bending the edges

ABRACADABRA. *Use your imagination and make your own.* Left to right: *Pedestal with cupholder, two compotes of stacked tin cans, copper pipe and tubing, baluster post, candle mold, two coffee tins soldered together, lamp base, metal pipe.* Center row. *Molded plumber's lead, air-conditioner filter wrapped around a tin can, chandelier part topped with a florist bowl, candlestick fitted with cupholder.* Front row. *Pyrex pie plate, painted; two tin boxes cemented together and covered with adhesive-backed paper; Pyrex baking dish, painted.* [SUTER]

to a depth necessary to build sides for a container. Lead is malleable enough to work with your hands, but it is more easily shaped when pounded with a hammer.

Bases

Whether or not to add a base is always a question. What can a base do for your design? Chosen wisely, a base can increase the importance of a design by setting it off on a platform; included without justification or when it is out of character, it can be a detriment. Sometimes exhibitors in flower shows use a base just for the sake of doing so, without regard for suitability for the overall effect.

Ten Ways a Base Contributes to Design

1. It can provide contrast of line and variation in form. It can counter a strongly vertical container or design with a horizontal line, or offset a round shape with one that is elongated.

2. It can sustain continuity through gradation of form and by repetition of characteristics, as mass, delicacy, or distortion, to the foot and conclusion of a design.

3. It can reinforce dominance by repeating color, texture, or shape.

4. It can introduce depth by directing the eye backward and forward.

5. It can moderate intensity by subduing bright colors and shiny textures.

6. It can improve proportion, increasing height of a container or of an arrangement too low for the space occupied.

7. It can promote rhythm by extending the flow of line.

8. It can introduce space by lifting a design above the table.

9. It can contribute visual stability by anchoring a design that appears deficient in bottom weight.

10. It can unify containers or objects that are separated, or change their levels to give variety.

Practically, a felt-backed base prevents damage to furniture from

ADD-A-BASE. *Camellia blossoms with foliage and fragrant garden viburnum are arranged in a hollowed-out driftwood container. The addition of a base improves proportion and balance, since the stand mounting the driftwood, though physically adequate, lacks visual weight to anchor the design.* [SUTER]

scratches and water leaks, and acts as a prop when fastened to a container or piece of driftwood enabling it to stand.

Generally, a container with a flat bottom looks better on a base than one elevated on a tripod of three feet or three legs.

A base coordinates with container and design when:

1. It harmonizes in color.

2. It is compatible in texture or material expressing the same tone of formality or informality.

3. It is related through style to period or national origin.

4. It corresponds in scale to the size of the components as well as the whole.

Bases are composed of bamboo, ceramic, cork, fabric, glass, marble, metal, plastic, slate, straw, Styrofoam, or wood; or they may be improvised from household trays. Many ready-made styles are available, some works of art in themselves.

In flower shows, a base is not an accessory, but is considered along with container, plant material, and background as an integral part of a design.

4

MASTERING MECHANICS

My mother was an accomplished arranger. She was always being asked to fix flowers for parties. It was a yearly tradition for her to make the centerpiece on opening day at the race track where her friends held a luncheon in the clubhouse to usher in the season. I remember her frustration on the first of these occasions when she arrived, flowers in hand, and found nothing to put them in but a glass bowl. She knew that a floral design without proper mechanics invites disaster. I don't know how my mother improvised, but you can be sure the following year she brought her own needle-holder and clay.

The mainstay of any floral design is the device that holds it together. Something must keep flowers in assigned positions and prevent their sliding around in the container, or worse still, falling out of it. You know what happens if you put a rose by itself in a glass of water. With nothing to prop it, the rose leans on the rim for support.

Needle-holders   The basic mechanics of arranging are so simple that with a 3-inch needle-holder, floral clay, and a shallow container, a beginner can easily make an acceptable design for living room or dining table on the first try. The art of composition begins with this limited equipment, the number of devices increasing as containers and construc-

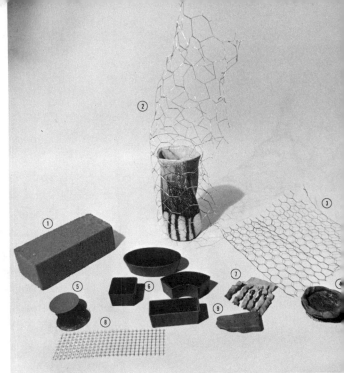

MECHANICS, STATIONING DEVICES OR HOLDERS.
1. Oasis. 2. Two-inch turkey wire mesh. 3. One-inch chicken wire mesh. 4. Upturned needle-holder with "worm" of clay around edge. 5. Two needle-holders, one turned over the other for weight. 6. Cupholders in various shapes. 7. Lead butterfly. 8. Hardware cloth. 9. Floral clay. [SUTER]

tion are diversified. A round needle-holder, 2½ to 3½ inches in diameter, has such varied uses that it should be a household staple. Besides accommodating almost any arrangement of average size, it is rustproof, reusable, and lasts almost indefinitely if properly cared for and not dropped on its face. However, just any kind of holder won't do. The best are heavy, lead-based, and with long sharp needles or pins set close together. These requirements are essential for a holder to remain fixed under the weight of plant materials and to keep them in place.

The stability of an arrangement depends on how firmly a holder is secured to a container. Reusable waterproof clay, made for the purpose, provides the adhesive; it holds fast even though submerged in water, and remains soft when not in use. Therefore no substitutes such as modeling clay or Silly Putty are acceptable, although in extreme cases chewing gum has been used. When you attach them—bowl, clay, and holder—even your hands must be absolutely dry. Never transfer mechanics from a wet to a dry container, for no matter how hard you press, the clay will not stick where there is moisture. Therefore, add water *after* the arrangement is completed, not before.

As your work becomes more complex, you will need holders in various sizes and shapes—round, oval, square, rectangular, and crescent—also in sets of two or three shapes interlocking to form different units. Holders are painted green, brown, or black, or come in a plain metal finish that can be sprayed to suit your design. Needle-holders are available from half an inch to 6 inches across.

The size of the holder is an important consideration, the quantity and weight of plant material the determining factor. A needle-holder must be heavy enough to balance the weight of an arrangement and large enough to accommodate the number and thickness of the stems. If it is too small, there will not be enough space to complete a design; if too large, some needles will remain exposed and have to be hidden with the usual aides of stones, foliage, or bits of driftwood. Means of concealment must be so skillful that they belie their purpose, appearing instead as part of the design. In flower shows, novices often lose points because they crowd superfluous scraps at the base of an arrangement to cover up a too-big holder. In traditional arrangements (particularly in competition), mechanics must not show. In modern designs, they may be visible if skillfully incorporated.

Occasionally needles are bent or spread apart when heavy branches are impaled. Needles can be straightened and debris removed from a holder with a Japanese gadget called a *kenzan*-straightener (*kenzan* is the Japanese equivalent for needle-holder).

Cupholders Comparable to a needle-holder is a cupholder, a small receptacle and needle-holder welded together. Though shallow, a cupholder can accommodate a sizable arrangement. It has a number of uses. Set on a base behind a rather large figurine, a piece of driftwood or rock, the cupholder can support plant material and supply water. It can also supply moisture in containers that do not hold water, or it can be exactly fitted to the opening of a tall vase for easier arranging.

Select weighty cupholders with closely set needles. Since cupholders are shallow, they must be sturdy enough to balance an arrangement prone to topple over. With walls less than 2 inches high, a cupholder has a small capacity for water, which is likely to evaporate overnight. Consequently, the supply must be replenished daily and sometimes even more frequently.

A cupholder centered on a candlestick converts this to a container when the two are attached with floral clay. For greater security, you can tie the holder onto the candlestick with florist wire (22-gauge). Cross two pieces, over the top, bring down below the candlecup, and twist around the shaft of candlestick. Still better is a device called an adapter, commercially an O-dapter, with a knob-like protrusion that fits into the opening made for the candle. (See photograph on page 63.) Since some adapters also have a place for a candle, you can include a candle in your arrangement if you wish. I have seen glass and plastic adapters but the kind I like best is brass.

Unfortunately, you can't always locate adapters since not all florists stock them, but you can improvise one. First anchor a needle-holder with clay to the inside of a small shallow tunafish, water-chestnut, or sliced pineapple can. Then attach the can to a candlestick with clay.

Stationing a Needle-holder

To fasten needle-holder and container together, roll a chunk of clay into a quarter-inch-thick "worm" long enough to fit the edge of an inverted holder. Lay the clay around the inside edge, then turn the holder right side up and press it with a twisting motion onto the container. Since seepage loosens contact, smear oozing clay around the edges for a watertight fit. To make sure the two won't separate, try lifting the container by the holder. My first teacher always inverted my completed arrangement and shook it gently to test mechanics. If anything fell out, or worse still, if the whole arrangement landed on the floor, I had to do over the design from the beginning. Although I have despised the whole business of mechanics ever since, the training was invaluable for constructing arrangements that remain intact when transported to a show.

If an arrangement or a branch in a shallow bowl is unusually heavy, it may overturn a needle-holder. To increase weight, invert a second holder over the first, placing the top one a little to the back or side with some teeth interlocking. The inverted holder gives balance and weight, yet leaves most of the needles on the bottom holder exposed for impaling stems.

Mechanics for Tall Containers

Needle-holders are best for shallow bowls and not-too-deep compotes. In tall vases, if the needle-holder rests on the bottom, arranging is difficult since stems cannot be inserted horizontally or at an angle. Only a vertical design can be constructed unless curved materials can be found to give breadth. The difficulty can be overcome by raising the floor of the container to within 3 or 4 inches of the top; this still allows for enough water to cover the holder and reach the stems. Several fillers serve the purpose—sand, which makes a heavy container heavier but weights a light one, wet crushed newspaper, or Kitty Litter, which is my preference. Dampened bird gravel is also recommended, but this is expensive as a small box of it doesn't go very far. (As mentioned earlier, you can set a cupholder in the top of a container, too.)

To make a level surface for the holder and prevent rocking, pour a layer of warm paraffin on top of the filler; when the wax begins to set, imbed the holder to the depth where base joins needles. Let the wax cool and harden. Take care to keep the paraffin from dripping onto the points lest you dull them; also avoid seepage between needles as this shortens the shafts and prevents penetration of stems. Once you have experienced the futility of trying to force flowers onto a clogged holder, you will take care thereafter. To guard against fire when you melt the paraffin, heat it in a tin can

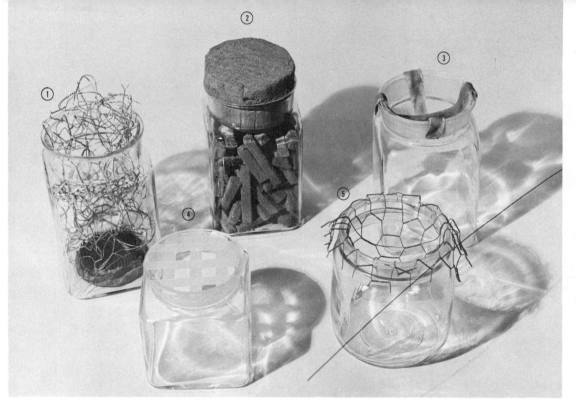

MECHANICS FOR TALL CONTAINERS. *1. Crumpled turkey wire, needle-holder and clay. 2. Oasis sticks and block. 3. Lead cross-bar sling, Oasis block inserted on top. 4. Scotch tape. 5. One-inch chicken-wire basket.* [SUTER]

set in a pan of water on top of the stove and keep constant watch. Paraffin is better for silver bowls than clay that stains the metal. Save leftover candles for a ready supply or use household canning wax.

Wire Netting Another mechanic for tall containers is the old standby, wire netting. Although either 2-inch turkey wire or 1-inch chicken wire can be used, the one with larger holes is recommended. When openings in the mesh are too small, there is insufficient room for stems and they get chewed, or become entangled, making removal difficult if positions must be changed. The larger netting is lighter in weight, more pliable, and kinder to hands. However, if 2-inch wire is not obtainable, chicken wire will suffice if crushed lightly. Since wire netting scratches, it is not advised for containers that are easily marred.

Netting is better than a needle-holder when you want to insert stems horizontally in a tall container. Netting also makes a better support for branches and stems too heavy for Oasis. Efficiency depends on the amount of mesh used; if too little, the plant material will squash it to the bottom of the vase, if too much, the netting will have to be squeezed to fit and then the holes will be closed.

Before you measure netting, cut off the hard selvage at each side with tin snips (don't ruin your flower scissors) and discard it. Cut the netting twice as long as the depth of the container; to determine the width needed, wrap the netting once around the vase and cut where the sides meet. Close it to make a long loose roll, no tighter than needed to wedge it into the vase. Once the wire is inserted, stretch the holes apart inside the container, keeping the wider openings through the center. To angle stems, dome the wire above the rim of the container. After you have fitted a vase with netting, leave it in place; then you need prepare each container only once and it is always ready for service. To prevent the wire from rusting, add a pinch of borax to the water in the vase before you start your arrangement.

For goblets, especially if stems are heavy, I like a combination of turkey wire and holder, for neither gives adequate support alone. A goblet is not deep enough to hold the mesh steady against the push and pull of plant materials, but if a holder is used instead, it is still too deep for angling stems. By using both holder and netting, the netting pressed onto the needles around the edge of the holder can support shorter stems, leaving most of the holder empty to grasp the stems that reach to the bottom of the goblet.

The same mechanics can be used in a large compote or a wide-mouth bowl for a massive arrangement. Cut the turkey wire not quite three times the diameter of the opening of the container. More will be needed for a deep than a shallow bowl. Crush the netting lightly by turning the edges in toward the center until you have a loose wad that just fits the opening.

At one time it was common practice to stuff a vase with evergreen clippings, jamming them in vertically like a bundle of hay, cutting the tips slightly below the rim of the container. Messy and unreliable, this method belongs at the bottom of the list and should only be used in an emergency if no other mechanics are available.

Oasis Most traditional arrangements look more graceful if flowers hang over the edge of the container. Floral foam or Oasis is the perfect mechanic here, as stems can be inserted at any angle, even upside down. However, it has two minor disadvantages. Once punctured, holes remain usually preventing reuse of the block, and water retention is limited to one night, at best, so water must be added daily. Brick-form Oasis should be cut to the exact size and shape of the container so as to fill the inside completely. A kitchen knife, toy saw, or length of wire held taut makes a good tool.

When you work with fresh flowers, soak the Oasis thoroughly in deep water before use. I keep extra wet blocks on hand in plastic bags that lock in moisture. The consequences of working with dry Oasis were embarrassingly illustrated by a speaker at one of our

FOR A CANDLECUP. *Mechanics convert candlestick to container and also anchor materials.* [KLENDER]

garden club meetings. Although a seasoned lecturer, she began constructing a table piece in a brittle block of Oasis, already punched with holes. She placed this in the center of a wide compote that gave it no support. When the design was almost completed, its weight split the dry Oasis down the center and each half with the flowers fell to the table.

Since this incident, I take extra precautions to prevent such a catastrophe. In a compote or candlecup, I anchor the needle-holder with clay. Next, I cover the needles with plastic torn from a cleaner's bag. On top, I press wet Oasis, already measured and cut to fit the sides of the container, but deeper so the Oasis will protrude up to an inch and a half above the rim. This lets me insert stems horizontally into the sides of the Oasis. Finally, I make a cage of 1-inch chicken wire cut to completely cover the Oasis and reach just below the rim of the container.

I tie the cage on with florist wire (22-gauge). This is woven through the holes of the mesh and encircles the compote. Sometimes I cross two more wires through the mesh over the top of the Oasis, tying them together underneath the bowl or to the wire threaded around the outside of the bowl. The plastic between Oasis and holder makes a liner that keeps the Oasis from clogging the needles. Digging out bits of Oasis is a tedious job to be avoided. Furthermore, if larger than the Oasis, the plastic sticks out so I can grasp the ends and easily pull the Oasis free when I need to replace it.

To measure Oasis, cut a block at least 2 inches longer than the depth of a container. Mark the width by pressing the end of the block onto the rim of the container. Then let the imprint guide you in cutting the sides. Press the Oasis into the container, then cut the top so it protrudes above the rim, as suggested above. If a container has thin walls, as those made of metal, you can simply press a wet block down into it without prior marking and cut away the surplus foam on the outside.

Oasis is also useful for dried arrangements. Since these are lightweight and stems are thin, the Oasis need not be moistened. To prevent weak stems from breaking when inserted, first poke holes in the Oasis with ice pick or wire in the exact places where each stem is to go to give it easy entrance. Oasis is also sold in sticks that can be stuffed into a container. Scraps and old blocks no longer usable can be salvaged and cut into small pieces for the same purpose. If you use Oasis sticks, pack them solidly into the container.

If you prefer Oasis to wire netting for a tall vase, stuff it about halfway to the top with Oasis sticks, adding water until this is completely absorbed. Then insert a solid block of Oasis and cover it with chicken wire as before. If you wish, you can tuck the ends of the chicken wire into the container instead of tying them to the outside. For this method, press Oasis and cage into the container at the same time.

With Oasis, plant materials must be well-hardened (see Chapter 5) or they are likely to wilt. Even so, some do not last in Oasis, notably anemones and gerberas whose stems become clogged; lilacs and various other woody branches may not receive enough moisture. It is better to limit these unreliable materials to arrangements that stand in water at least 2 to 3 inches deep.

Do no confuse Oasis with Styrofoam. Although they are similar, Styrofoam is a hard substance that does not absorb water. It is unsuitable for fresh materials, but makes a fine holder for dried ones.

For Glass Containers

In tall transparent glass containers, a holder and stems that show spoil the design. In shallow bowls, mechanics can often be hidden by foliage overhanging the rim in front. Generally, the mechanics I have discussed are not suitable for glass. In fact, most arrangers avoid glass. If you must use it, the best device is a lead-butterfly. Although this is seldom available commercially you can easily make your own from plumber's sheet lead.

To construct a lead-butterfly, cut a 3 by 4-inch rectangle of lead with tin snips. Fringe it into 6 half-inch strips 3¼ inches long, leaving a ¾-inch solid band at the top. (See photo page 57.)

To clamp the butterfly onto the container, bend the two outside strips over the outer rim. Bend up the inside strips and twist them around the stems, which can then be cut off just below the butterfly. No other holder is necessary.

Or you can shape strips of lead into a sling for a needle-holder. Cut two ¾-inch-wide strips long enough to cross the mouth of the vase, thus making a U-shaped sling. Set this low enough for water to reach the stems. Hook the four ends of the strips over the rim of the container. The same type of sling can be made from hardware cloth. (See photo page 61.)

A basket made of chicken wire also makes a good supporting device for Oasis in a glass container. The basket reminds me of a kitchen sieve. To construct it, cut a section the shape of the mouth of the vase wide enough for edges of the mesh to hook over the outside rim of the container, and also make a well when pushed down in the center. The bottom of the basket should reach below the level of the water. To keep the mesh from slipping, lace florist wire (22-gauge) through the holes of the mesh around the outside of the container; where ends meet, twist them together.

For lightweight materials with thin stems, make a lattice of Scotch tape across the top of a container. Openings between crossings should be wide enough to admit several stems through each. (This method has been saved for last because I like it least.)

Other Aids Even with the best mechanics, there are problems. Stems may split, be too tough to impale, too thin or too soft to take hold, too weak to stand alone; some short when you need them long, others straight when you want curves, or the reverse. Flowers and leaves may need adjustment. Heavy heads droop; blossoms may open too far or not far enough. Leaves you want slightly curled may be ramrod straight. Here are some tricks that make manipulation easier.

To Angle a Heavy Branch. *Insert the branch upright on the holder; draw the branch down to the desired angle.* [KLENDER]

TO INSERT STEMS ON A NEEDLE-HOLDER

1. Cut stems on a slant to provide a larger surface for water intake and also make penetration of needles easier.

2. For woody or other tough stems difficult to impale, make crisscross cuts in the ends as deep as the length of the needles; push onto holder.

3. To angle a branch, insert it in an upright position; then exert pressure at the base to draw the branch down to a slanting position.

4. To force tough woody stems onto a holder or stakes for fastening fruits and vegetables, tap with a small hammer. (See Chapter 14.)

TO REINFORCE STEMS

1. For thin stems of freesias, sweet peas, pansies, etc., bunch three or four stems together, tie with wire (22-gauge), and insert as one.

2. To strengthen a hollow stem and obtain a better hold at the base, insert wire (18-gauge) the length of the stem or insert a piece of iris or gladiolus stalk into the hollow stem.

3. To brace a heavy branch or flower stem, impale it on a holder,

then hammer beside it a short green stake of privet and wire the two together or use a Twist-Em.

TO REPAIR STEMS

1. To prop a droopy head, insert a wire (18-gauge) through the top of the bloom and push the wire into the stem. Cut off excess wire at the top and push the cut end down out of sight into flower head.

2. To bind a fleshy stem that splits and curls, wrap the base with floral tape or a Twist-Em, taking care not to stop up the stem opening (for calla-lily).

3. To rescue a bent stem, insert wire (18-gauge) up through it.

4. To mend a broken stem, splint it with wire (18-gauge), or if it is heavy, tape the stem to a stake for the length of the stem.

TO LENGTHEN STEMS SO AS TO ELEVATE FLOWERS

1. Wire (22-gauge) the short stem to the needed length of: ¼-inch balsa wood stick, green privet stake or similar sturdy shrub, bamboo stake, florist pick, or stalk of gladiolus or iris.

2. Wire an orchid tube or metal cone to one of the above "stretchers" for very short stems of flowers that must be in water. Impale the stick onto the needle-holder.

TO MAKE STEMS CURVE

1. For a hollow stem, push a wet pipe cleaner up into the stem as far as the flower head (for daffodils). For a solid stem, insert a wire (18-gauge) and bend gently (for gerbera, tulips).

2. For a thin stem, cut to desired length, pierce bloom at base with wire (18-gauge) and tape wire to length of stem. This also reinforces. To wrap floral tape, wind it a few turns around a stem and wire. Hold the stem in your right hand, twirling as you stretch tape with your left. This makes wrapping secure especially if tape is allowed to overlap as it is wound.

3. For a soft stem, insert wire (18-gauge) into the base of the flower head, then wrap the wire around the stem down to the end, giving the wire a few extra turns at the bottom. For carnations, insert wire into blooms to prop up heads.

4. To bend a branch without breaking it, grasp it between your hands keeping them close together, thumbs touching. Bend gradually, moving your hands as a unit up and down the stem. If your hands spread apart while you are exerting pressure, the branch is likely to snap in two. This works well for pussy willow, winged euonymus, plum, etc.

TO PREVENT FLOWERS FROM OPENING OR SHATTERING

1. Spray with floral glue or floral adhesive.

2. With a small paintbrush, seal edges of petals with egg white diluted with a little water or use Elmer's glue (for tulips, roses).

3. Drop heated candle wax or paraffin into the center to keep water-lilies open; to the outside base of chrysanthemums to prevent shattering.

TO SHAPE LEAVES

1. Soak in warm water for an hour to soften to workable condition.

2. Lay wire (18-gauge) along back of midrib, and fasten with Scotch tape or green floral adhesive tape; then curve leaf gently (for ti leaves, aspidistra). With fleshy leaves, insert wire up into the midrib (for canna, sansevieria).

3. Loop or make ribbons of leaves by curling around index and third finger and clamp loop in place with a hand stapler (for gladiolus, yucca).

4. Roll leaves lengthwise or furl forward or backward; fasten with Scotch tape, stapler, or short hairpin of wire (22-gauge), and twist shut (for ti leaves).

5. Make rosettes of leaves from ivy and galax by clustering three or four and tying stems together.

The Tool Kit

NECESSITIES

Flower shears (6-inch size) made for arranging, not gardening. The Japanese wide-handle or butterfly scissors is recommended.
Needle-holder, round, 2½ to 3½ inches in diameter
Floral clay

OTHER AIDS

Balsa wood sticks or bamboo stakes
Baster from kitchen for adding water to cupholder—it gives better control than a watering can and avoids spilling
Bucket for gathering and hardening flowers and foliage

TOOL KIT. 1. *Child's saw.* 2. *Small Japanese saw.* 3. *Stapler.* 4. *Pipe cleaners.* 5. *Kitchen baster.* 6. *Japanese butterfly scissors.* 7. *Tin snips.* 8. *18-gauge wire.* 9. *Balsa wood sticks.* 10. *Mister or sprayer.* 11. *Paring knife.* 12. *22-gauge wire.* 13. *Florist picks.* 14. *Combination pliers and wire cutter.* 15. *Floral tape.* 16. *Orchid tubes.* 17. *Ice pick.* 18. *Small hammer.* 19. *Twist-Ems.* 20. *Needle-holder and straightener.* [SUTER]

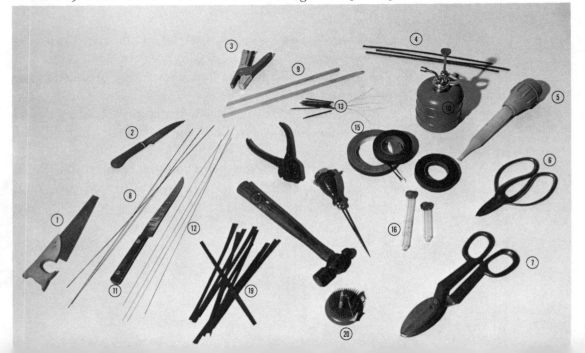

Chicken wire (1-inch)

Floral adhesive tape

Floral glue

Floral tape, both green and brown

Florist wire (18- and 22-gauge)

Hammer (small)

Hardware cloth, for positioning branches of weathered wood

Ice pick, for piercing fruits and vegetables to be wired or making holes in Oasis for inserting weak stems

Knife, kitchen, medium size, for cutting stems on a slant before placing in deep water to harden

Needle-holders and cupholders in assorted sizes and shapes

Kenzan straightener (with pick) for straightening needles and cleaning holder

Oasis or plastic foam blocks

Orchid tubes for raising flowers in arrangements and inserting blooms and foliage between fruits and vegetables when no container is used

Paraffin

Pegs, cut from branches of green wood, also forked or Y-shaped pieces for fastening grapes and other fruits and vegetables

Pipe cleaners

Pliers for twisting wires

Plumber's sheet lead

Saw (small Japanese) for cutting heavy branches

Saw (toy), for cutting Oasis

Sprayer, commercial type for flowers or window-spray bottle with atomizer for misting arrangement with water to keep it fresh

Stapler (hand) and staples

Stones, to conceal holder

Styrofoam, for arranging dried materials or plastic flowers

Tool caddy, box, or wicker basket, for storing tools

Turkey wire (2-inch mesh)

Twist-Em or plant ties
Wire cutter or tin snips

EXTRAS

Screwdriver
Scotch tape
Scissors (small for intricate trimming)
Straight pins

5

HOW TO KEEP THEM FRESH

At the time of my oldest son's graduation from high school, two other mothers and I volunteered to take charge of Italian night, one of the June Week festivities. We were responsible for the table decorations; one parent would provide Chianti bottles for containers, another would bring peonies from her garden, and I was elected to arrange them.

I arrived early the night of the dinner followed by the mother bringing the flowers, her arms full of droopy peonies wrapped in newspapers. Obviously she was upset, puzzled that the open blossoms she had cut less than an hour ago were already wilted. Since she had always depended on a florist for centerpieces, she had never learned a cardinal rule of arranging: few plant materials will keep fresh unless they have been hardened beforehand. That evening I introduced her to an almost foolproof method of rescuing flagging blooms. Filling a sink with warm water, I doused the flowers, blossoms and all, then recut the stems *under* water and let them remain there for almost half an hour for a long drink. They revived and our centerpieces were a success.

Proper Tools and Cutting

For material to stay fresh, it must first be cut properly and then conditioned. The first step requires proper tools. Steel flower clippers designed solely for arranging are essential. More expensive than kitchen scissors, they are worth the cost since they can sever all but tree limbs almost as readily as delicate stems, and the short, strong blades are so sharp they minimize damage to plant cells. You can determine the quality of clippers by how well they cut a heavy branch. When leverage is applied to the handles of a good pair, a woody stem will not slip out of the crotch to the front of the blades as they close. Household scissors cannot grasp stems of even lighter weight and fail to cut stout ones. There are several dependable flower shears on the market; I like the Japanese butterfly scissors (6 inches overall length), so-called because the wide loops of the handles suggest the spread wings of a butterfly.

Although clippers are favored for arranging and cutting from the garden, and are essential for branches, a sharp kitchen knife of medium size is better for the next step of preparing flower stems for conditioning. When materials are brought indoors (or home from a florist), stems should be recut *on a slant* to expose a wide surface for absorption. If stems are cut straight across, the ends will rest squarely on the bottom of a container and so reduce water intake. A sharp knife is also efficient for removing thorns from roses. If the stem is held horizontally, the cut end toward you, the knife blade, pulled down the length of the stem from flower to base, scrapes the stem clean.

Conditioning in Deep Water

The procedure for hardening is the same for florist as for garden material. When you transport flowers and foliage, take a water-filled pail with you. And if you sometimes drive in the country, keep one in the car along with your flower scissors; then you will be prepared for any material you see that is worth collecting but that cannot endure even a brief period of dryness, as Queen-Anne's-lace. In fact, this roadside weed is so wilt-prone that when I plan to dry it, I take a box of borax and cornmeal mixture in the car and bury the blooms immediately after cutting. (For drying, see Chapter 12.)

In general, the best times for cutting flowers from the garden are

SPRING ARRANGEMENT. *Flowering branches and tulips last longer if materials are properly hardened.* [SUTER]

early in the morning when plants are turgid with dew or late in the afternoon, after they have built up a supply of food and manufactured energy. Since plants transpire most during the heat of the day (especially in summer), the middle of the afternoon is the poorest time, unless the weather is cool, rainy, or cloudy; then you can cut at any time. Take the pail with you to the garden, and indoors re-cut stems on a slant immediately, removing all foliage that would rest below the water. If leaves remain under water, they decay creating matter that clogs stems.

As each stem is prepared, it should be quickly returned to clean water reaching halfway up to the flower. When soaked for several hours or overnight, materials absorb enough moisture to sustain them for several days in your arrangements. Since flowers wilt when evaporation takes place faster than water is absorbed, it is essential

PREPARING ROSES. *Scrape thorns from stem by holding it head-down and drawing paring knife toward you.* [SUTER]

to reduce transpiration (loss of moisture) and increase humidity. Immersing stems up to the bloom helps.

When I am preparing for a party or a flower show, I like to make my arrangement the night before. I buy or cut materials the morning of the previous day and let them harden until after supper when I begin to work. When the design is completed, I spray it well with cool water and set it in the cooler garage for the night. Early next morning, I add more water, if any has evaporated, and mist the whole thing. Before transporting to a show, I spray again. For a party, I spray once or twice more during the day. Late in the afternoon, I set the arrangement on the dining table, open the window a crack, pull down the shades, and close the door until dinner time.

Water Temperature

There are various theories as to the best water temperature—warm or hot, cool or cold. I consulted a professor of botany (who wishes to remain anonymous). Based on his knowledge of plant physiology, he offered a common-sense approach, emphasizing that all plants do not react the same way; some require specific treatment. For most garden plants, he advises against hot water because the metabolism of plants is stimulated by heat. When metabolism occurs, roots are supplying food. If metabolism (a complicated process of building up food and breaking down waste) starts *after* cutting, a plant uses up the energy it has stored in leaves and stems and has no means of replacing it. The consequences are wilting, even death.

Except for tropical material, the professor advises cool, even icy, water which slows down metabolism. In cold water, the cut plant is not forced to deplete its reserves, transpiration is reduced, and stems are better able to take up moisture. Furthermore, tissues of plants cut in the garden dry out in two or three minutes unless stems are *immediately* put into cool water.

In arrangements, materials are subject to further risks of heat, light, drafts, and often inadequate moisture, and these conditions speed up transpiration. When flowers or foliage are in a state of *temporary* wilt due to these conditions, they should be placed in *warm* or *hottish* water, the stems recut under water. In this instance, warm water is used deliberately to induce metabolism, but once plants have been revived, they should be transferred to cool water to slow down consumption of energy.

Plants may also wilt from lack of nutrients; a small amount of sugar (1 teaspoon or less per quart) or a few drops of honey (1 teaspoon per gallon) may be added to the water to compensate. But don't add more, as too much sweetening causes osmosis, again "stimulating the use of energy," and this aggravates wilting. Here are the professor's recommendations for conditioning garden materials:

1. Use clean receptacles—bucket, container, and holder—to prevent development of bacteria.

2. Take a bucket of cool water to the garden to immerse stems within the crucial two or three minutes after cutting.

3. Indoors, recut stems on a slant; remove leaves that would rest below the water line. Return stems to deep, cool water.

4. Mist blooms with water, or submerge blossom as well as stem for a minute in cool water, drain, and cover with plastic.

5. Store for several hours or overnight in a cool, dark place away from drafts; if you have a spare refrigerator, turn to the lowest setting and keep your flowers there.

Note: Don't dunk flowers and foliage that would be damaged by submergence, as lamb's-ears (*Stachys*) or pansies. Instead, mist such materials with a woolly or velvety texture and then cover with plastic. Check to be sure moisture is not collecting on blossoms or leaves; should this occur, lift plastic for several minutes so air can circulate, and partially dry the plastic.

For Foliage and Woody Branches

The structure of a plant determines resistance to wilting. Although all leaves last better if given a long drink of water, some kinds transpire so quickly that unless water is supplied *immediately* after cutting, they go limp at once. Some plants from hot climates, like bird-of-paradise and ti, have self-protection against fast transpiration, but evaporation is rapid from the foliage of hosta, calla-lily, castor bean, begonia, ligularia, horseradish, and some others. These are handicapped by large leaf surfaces exposed to air. However, those broad surfaces can also absorb water. Submerging the whole leaf in cool water for several hours or overnight facilitates intake and foliage becomes firm and crisp, able to survive a day or two in an arrangement. But, there is a difference between a saturated and a water-logged leaf. If foliage stays under water too long, it rots and the damage is irreparable.

Certain plants, such as aspidistra, ivy, monstera, sansevieria, and yucca, tolerate lack of moisture and only the stems need be steeped for several hours or overnight. Wisteria foliage benefits from immersion. Needled and broadleaf evergreen branches transpire slowly with little loss of moisture; they keep well even under stress, but they benefit if stems are soaked. Desiccation can be further retarded if a tablespoon of glycerine is added to each quart of water. This treatment also helps prevent freezing of evergreens in outdoor decorations.

To prepare woody branches or tough stems like those of stock for better absorption, make 2-inch or deeper crosscuts into the base of stems; shorter cuts for shorter stems. When trees and shrubs are being used primarily for foliage, don't remove below-water leaves that might be useful, but do pick off defective leaves. For foliage material, water need not be as deep as for flowers but soaking time is the same. Depth of water varies with the length of branches but should be at least 5 inches.

Determining
Freshness

Sometimes flowers don't last for the simple reason that they aren't fresh to begin with. When you buy, be sure you are getting fresh merchandise. Notice leaves. They show signs of age by yellowing and flopping. When fresh, they are firm and most of them a healthy green. To test chrysanthemums, delphinium, and larkspur, shake gently to see if petals fall, and needled evergreens to determine shedding. With chrysanthemums and snapdragons, stems snap off sharply if they are fresh but require twisting if the peak is past. (When hardening chrysanthemums and snapdragons, I break the stems instead of cutting them.) Tulips and lilies cannot be snapped but must be cut, and take care not to break carnation stems at a node for then they are unable to drink.

It is wise to buy flowers in bud stage; they last longer and will, of course, open soon enough in a heated room. Refuse gladiolus if all the florets are open; instead, choose spikes with two florets open and all others just showing color. If you set them in warm water and leave them overnight where it is warm, more florets will be open by morning. As lower blossoms fade, remove them; new ones will open above, extending the life of gladiolus beyond that of most other flowers.

If you require special material and all that is available has evidently been in the shop for a while, insist on a generous reduction in price, or suggest, since it is not saleable that the florist give it to you as a gesture of goodwill and so insure your future patronage.

When gathering flowers from the garden, avoid those past their prime. Decline manifests itself in faded color, browning, or limpness on the reverse of petals. Age is indicated by the presence of yellow pollen specks in the center of flowers (zinnias), or capsules exposing seeds (celosia); loss of vigor is apparent if petals are thin, papery, or almost transparent. To get the best performance, pick flowers with clear, bright color, lustrous texture, and a certain resiliency.

For Problem Plants — Various treatments have been suggested to prolong the life of problem plants. Aspirin is now outmoded and ingredients that require a doctor's prescription are hardly practical, as "a pinch of zinc sulphate crystals in water to prevent decay of stems and foliage of marigolds."

Actually, just soaking stems in cool, deep water results in perky marigolds that last a week. To keep water fresh for any flowers for several days, Mrs. Edward Maher, a Maryland horticulturist, recommends adding a few drops of Clorox.

To prevent dahlias from collapsing, potassium nitrate has been advocated, also burning stem ends. But Mrs. J. Edgar Miller, a dahlia authority and grower, does not find that this retards wilting; it only damages tissues and so prevents water intake. She cuts dahlias in their prime, or slightly past, and never in bud as they wilt then. Indoors, she recuts stems on a slant with a sharp knife and soaks the stems in *warm* water for several hours or overnight. So treated, dahlias keep fresh for several days and may even be boxed and taken dry to a show several hours away. After transporting, flowers should be placed in *lukewarm* water. If dahlias are not fully open when cut, standing stems in hot water encourages petal spread, but at this stage, there is some risk of wilting. (*Note:* The dahlias photographed in this book, many of which came from Mrs. Miller's garden, were hardened according to her directions and lasted from four to six days.)

For advice on some other difficult to hold flowers, I consulted Mrs. Toku M. Sugiyama, Executive Director of the Sogetsu School, U.S.A. She has no trouble with euphorbia and other flowers exuding a milky sap or hydrangeas if she recuts the stems under water (to check the flow of fluid) and then dips the cut ends in alum in the jar just as she buys it from the drugstore. She also keeps ornamental grasses from wilting by standing stems for a few minutes in undiluted vinegar while she makes an arrangement. From Mrs. C. Albert Standiford, former Horticulture District Chairman for the Federated Garden Clubs of Maryland, I got a helpful tip on keeping daylilies open for a dinner party. Cut them in the morning when they are closed and place in water in a refrigerator, hopefully one that will not be opened frequently. On the table at dinner time, the flowers open and stay open for their normal eight-hour period.

(In the refrigerator the flowers think it's nighttime, under electric light in the dining room they think it's day.) This procedure is worth trying with other flowers that close at night.

Other suggestions for problem plants involve boiling stems, soaking them in solutions of red pepper, salt, vinegar, weak tea, tobacco, or Japanese rice wine, better known as sake, or rubbing stems with alcohol or peppermint oil.

Here are treatments I have found practical.

Bamboo. Drill a hole down through the stem to open nodes, or drill a hole below each node and inject water into each one.

Buddleia, lilac, mock-orange. Remove *all* foliage, split stems, stand in deep water overnight.

Celosia, daffodils. Set in *shallow* water to avoid waterlogging.

Lilies. Pull off stamens to prevent pollen from staining petals, table linen, or other surfaces.

Lotus leaves. Lotus leaves will not wilt if you prevent air from entering the stem. Cut the stem under water and, while the cut end is still submerged, place your finger over the opening as you remove it from the water. Holding your finger in place, invert the stem (above water), lift your finger, and quickly fill the stem with pond water from a kitchen baster, which should already be full and waiting. Replace your finger and continue to use as a stopper to prevent water from leaking out as you turn the stem right side up and place it under water again in a bucket. Now, you can have back your finger! (This useful procedure was worked out by Malcolm W. Lowenstein.)

When I glycerinize lotus leaves, I have the solution beside me and inject it into the stems instead of pond water; then I stand the stems in the glycerine solution. With this method, leaves turn a soft tan and remain pliable. They take several weeks to cure. (Mine are two years old and still in good condition.) Take care that no air enters the stem after cutting for then the process is useless. (For glycerinizing, see Chapter 12.)

Peony. Cut single and Japanese types when less than half open; cut doubles when top of bud feels soft like a marshmallow. Kept in a refrigerator, peonies will not open, and can be held back for a week to ten days.

Tulips. To keep stems straight, wrap them in newspaper reaching up to the flowers and stand in deep water.

Unless they are notorious for wilting, you will find that most flowers perform well after normal hardening in water. Since remedies vary widely for difficult plant materials, it is impractical to suggest here a number of specific solutions. In general, soaking stems in water and then storing flowers in a refrigerator beats all other methods, but don't store with apples; these give off ethylene gas injurious to blooms.

Flower Shows

In flower shows, wilted materials preclude an award regardless of the caliber of the design. Although flowers and foliage need not be quality horticulture specimens, they must indeed look fresh. It makes no difference to judges that an arrangement was in fine condition when it was placed. If it has gone limp between the time it was entered and the hour for evaluation, it is still judged as seen. In this regard, judges are without mercy; in fact, especially in large shows, judges may look for evidence that a design will last through the exhibition; if it appears that later in the day the public will be viewing a drooping prize winner, an award may be withheld.

When you enter a competition, do obtain materials early enough to condition them, and allow a few extras for emergency. A stem may break in transport, petals can be damaged. If the replacement is a bloom that you rushed out and picked at the last moment, it might not hold up for the two hours that just might elapse until the judges reached your class. It is wise to use materials you know are reliable and unlikely to ruin your chances by wilting. In a situation where a show lasts more than one day, exhibitors are expected to freshen

BURSTING INTO BLOOM. *Forced in winter, fragrant winterhazel makes a naturalistic setting for a figurine of a fisherman hauling in his catch.* [COPE]

designs by adding water on succeeding days and to replace any flagging material.

Forcing Branches

In winter, dormant flowering branches can be forced into bloom in the house. The procedure is similar to that for hardening material. Branches are ready for forcing after a hard freeze. Generally, the closer a plant is to its normal blooming time, the shorter the period for forcing. Select branches with the most buds for these will provide the greatest show in flower. Flower buds are larger and fatter than leaf buds, an easy means of differentiation. Try to cut on a mild day when temperatures are in the forties to fifties. Split stems, set in a bucket of warm water where the air is warm (but not so hot that buds dry out as they would near a radiator), and mist occasionally. The rest is a matter of waiting for nature to take its course—from several days to several weeks, depending on the time of year branches are cut and also on their nature.

These are some of the best woody plants for forcing: corylopsis (winterhazel), dogwood, flowering fruit trees (crab apple, peach, pear, plum, quince), forsythia, pussy willow, red maple, and witchhazel.

6

FOUR STEP-BY-STEP DESIGNS

Anyone can arrange flowers. Right from the start, simple arrangements are within the grasp of anyone who will follow a few guidelines.

Designing with flowers is a creative process, each design an experiment in relationships among colors, forms, and textures. As personal expression, flower arranging is fun and stimulating; each attempt brings a new challenge and fresh results. In searching for ways to present the usual in an unusual way, you will sharpen your perception, discovering design potential in objects and materials you never noticed before.

Making a composition of flowers and foliage is easy if you think of your first arrangement as an exclamation point—a continuing line of movement and a stopping place. Visualize the exclamation as a design with plant materials—a branch of upright yew with a peony at its base, a sansevieria leaf pointing up from an aucuba rosette that anchors the leaf to the container, or a gladiolus spike rising above a large chrysanthemum. Such a design can be made in seconds with little effort and no experience. Think of colors and textures that would look attractive in a composition with but one piece of plant material for line and another one for a round form. Work quickly. Inevitably the result will be pleasing, and you will be ready to try these four designs.

STEP-BY-STEP DESIGNS

Here are some guides, not rules to be followed rigidly. In collecting materials, try to include two or three pieces with strong line for foundation and framework and enough large round forms for focus. Add a few extra pieces of filler as these often come in handy for closing gaps and finishing the back of a design. Cut stems longer than you think you will need. And don't overlook buds. If you are using a container of a different size, adjust the plant measurements to the proportions given.

The first two arrangements show how a series of more complex designs can be developed by adding a new kind of material each time. However, beginning with Design Two the arrangement is complete in itself unless you wish to elaborate it.

Design One—
Vertical

MATERIALS

Low rectangular container 12 inches long, 8 inches wide, 2 inches deep
Round needle-holder, 3 inches in diameter
Floral clay
Six yucca leaves
Two rhododendron leaf clusters on short stems
Four branches arborvitae
Five tulips
Optional: Base, 15 inches long, 10 inches wide

DIRECTIONS

1. Center holder near back wall of container.
2. Cut yucca leaf to 20 inches for main line. Insert in holder back of center. Position leaf with tip pointing straight up over point of insertion. Check balance.

3. Cut second leaf to 19 inches. Place at left of main line slightly overlapping it in front.

4. Cut third leaf to 17 inches. Place to right of main line and slightly behind it.

5. Cut fourth leaf to 15 inches for reinforcing line. Place directly in front of main line.

6. Cut two yucca leaves to 14 and 12 inches each for side placements. Place one at each side slightly overlapping front of second and third leaves.

7. Choose two rhododendron branches with leaf clusters of different size, one about 10 inches across, the other 7 inches. Cut stem of smaller cluster to 9 inches. Cut stem to 4 inches for larger cluster. Remove leaves below each cluster. When the length of the top leaf of the cluster is included, the overall length will be approximately 13 inches for the longer branch, 9 inches long for the shorter branch.

8. Place cluster on taller branch left of center in front of yucca

DESIGN ONE.
Steps 1 through 6. Tallest leaf fixes height, balance, and central axis. Other leaves closely grouped and graduated in height fill in frame of design. [KLENDER]

Steps 7 and 8. Rhododendron varies form and creates focus. [KLENDER]

grouping, facing the cluster toward the right. Place shorter branch right of center, bending slightly forward and facing cluster toward left. The two clusters should look toward each other.

9. Cut four branches arborvitae, two, 9 inches; two, 10 inches long. Place two taller ones behind yucca leaves; place shorter branches, one at each side toward front, angling stems down to allow foliage to brush over rim of container.

10. Cut five tulips in different heights from 6 to 12 inches. Place the tallest behind leaves of tallest cluster following the center line of yucca. Place second tallest tulip below the left front corner of container. If you wish, reflex petals of center tulip a little to obtain a stronger focal area.

SUBSTITUTE PLANTS:

For yucca: Gladiolus, iris, or sansevieria foliage
For rhododendron: Photinia, sweet bay magnolia
For tulips: Anemones, daffodils

Step 9. Arborvitae increases fullness, adding filler and softening. [KLENDER]

Step 10. Completed Design. Tulips contribute color and further interest. [KLENDER]

Design Two—
Asymmetrical Right
Angle or L-Shape

MATERIALS

Low round bowl, approximately 11 inches in diameter, 2 inches
   deep
Needle-holder, 3 inches in diameter
Floral clay
Three long branches of juniper, two shorter ones
Two branches leatherleaf viburnum
Four gladiolus
Two large chrysanthemums or peonies
Optional: One round or irregularly shaped base, 15 inches in diam-
   eter

DIRECTIONS

1. Place holder toward left rear of container.

2. Choose a strong juniper branch with tip curving slightly to
right.

3. Cut branch 20 to 22 inches. Place at back of holder, left of
center. Face branch toward right with tip just above center of
holder. Check balance.

4. Cut reinforcing line of juniper 18 to 20 inches. Place in front
of main line.

5. Cut juniper to 17 inches for horizontal line of right angle.
Place horizontally at right, but high enough to clear rim of container.

6. Cut fourth branch of juniper to 12 inches. Slant at a 75-degree
angle between main and horizontal lines.

7. Cut two short branches of leatherleaf viburnum, 6 and 7
inches long, each with several leaves near the tip. Place in front to
flank main line, slanting outward at each side. Let leaves fan out.

8. Cut one gladiolus stalk to 16 inches, measuring at tip from
first bud showing color. Remove remaining top growth. (Measure
all gladiolus this way.) Pinch out lowest floret if it falls below water

DESIGN TWO · *Steps 1 through 6. Main branch to side and back of container establishes asymmetrical balance, assured by placement of tip directly above point of stem insertion. Side branches continue formation of asymmetrical triangle.* [KLENDER]

Step 7. Leatherleaf viburnum relieves fuzziness of juniper by addition of broad leaves, a different form. [KLENDER]

line. If florets are large, also pinch out one near center to relieve crowding.

9. Cut reinforcing gladiolus to 14 inches. Place stem directly in front of first gladiolus, but slant tip toward right.

10. Cut third gladiolus to 13 inches. (Use one that is curved if you have it.) Place in horizontal position in front of horizontal line of juniper.

11. Without moving stems, gently draw viburnum leaves from behind gladiolus blossoms to positions in front.

12. Cut fourth gladiolus to 10 inches. Place to follow horizontal stalk, slanting the tip slightly up. Remove any interfering florets from stems in back.

13. If you wish to complete the design at this stage, from left-over clippings, cut one short gladiolus stalk with two florets. Place

Steps 8 through 12. Placement of gladiolus follows and flowers strengthen foundation lines. [KLENDER]

Steps 13 through 16. Completed Design. Chrysanthemums, closely grouped, provide a strong center of interest with texture similar to juniper but contributing new form. [KLENDER]

low in front at center and finish at the bottom with short sprigs of juniper.

14. To continue design, omit step 13. Cut stems of two large chrysanthemums or peonies to 6 and 7 inches. Center taller one facing toward left. Slant shorter one facing outward toward right.

15. Cut a 10-inch branch of juniper. Place low at left of chrysanthemums pointing down toward the left side of bowl.

16. Close any gaps and finish at bottom with clippings of juniper.

SUBSTITUTE PLANTS:

For juniper: Cypress, yew
For leatherleaf viburnum: Aucuba, southern magnolia
For gladiolus: Ginger, plumed celosia
For chrysanthemums: Dahlias, ornamental cabbage or kale, peonies

Design Three—
Symmetrical
Triangle

MATERIALS

Pedestal or compote-type container, 6 to 7 inches high, 5 inches in
    diameter, 2 inches deep
Needle-holder, 3 inches in diameter
Floral clay
Ten bells-of-Ireland, some curving
Eleven to 14 asters
Eight stems sweet peas

DIRECTIONS

1. Choose a sturdy, well-tapered stalk of bells-of-Ireland. Cut to
16 inches. Insert two-thirds back on holder with tip pointing up in
line with point of stem insertion. Remove all florets below rim of
container and those that will interfere with other stems to be placed
front. Check balance.

2. Cut two stalks that curve toward each other, each to 9 inches.
Insert one at each side, at 75-degree angle to form corners of triangle. Tips should curve slightly forward.

3. Cut two stalks to 13 inches. Insert to right and left in back of
main line.

4. Cut reinforcing stalk to 14 inches. Place in front of main line.

5. Cut four more stalks, graduating heights to fill in, two on each
side between top and sides of triangle.

6. Begin to block in focal area with asters following lines of
frame, superimposing pattern on pattern. Reserve larger flowers for
central focus.

7. Cut first aster stem to 9 inches. Position in front to follow main
line.

8. Cut two side aster placements, each to 7 inches. Place at a
slightly forward angle at each side to follow horizontal line at base
of triangle, heads turned toward center of design.

Steps 1 through 3. Center and side placements estab-lish frame of symmetrical triangle. [KLENDER]

Steps 4 and 5. Additional bells-of-Ireland fill in frame. [KLENDER]

DESIGN THREE

Steps 6 through 9. Asters form a second smaller tri-angle based on lines of the first triangle. [KLENDER]

Steps 10 through 12. Completed Design. Filling in is an easy matter of following main structural lines. [KLENDER]

9. Cut the next two aster stems to 6 inches. Place along same line as step 8 above, to draw the design toward the center.

10. Continue closing in center area with asters by graduating the heights. Vary the direction of the heads.

11. For depth, add one or two asters in profile on each side at back.

12. Fill in with sweet peas of varying heights for transition and softening between elongated and round forms.

SUBSTITUTE PLANTS:

For bells-of-Ireland: Liatris, snapdragons, stock
For asters: Carnations, roses
For sweet peas: Boxwood, freesias, statice

Design Four— Horizontal, for a Centerpiece— Symmetrical

MATERIALS*

Candlestick, 16 inches high

Candlecup holder, or tuna fish can fitted with needle-holder. The holder helps to anchor Oasis and any stems that pierce through Oasis to the bottom

Floral clay to station holder in candlecup or can and anchor can onto candlestick

Small piece of plastic to put between Oasis and needles to keep them clean

Round block of Oasis cut to fit cup or can and extend 1 inch above rim

One-inch chicken wire cut as a cage to fit over Oasis and tied to cup with wire

Four long curving ivy sprays. Four or more shorter branches, some curling up, others down

A few large leaves of ivy or small sprays

* Plant materials indicated are sufficient to fill out the design for all-round viewing; for front viewing only, less will be needed.

Step 1. (See Chapter 4, p. 56 and photo on page 57 for illustration of mechanics.) Here are types of materials needed for main placements. [KLENDER]

Steps 2 through 5. In a horizontal design, proportion is determined not according to height, as in vertical composition, but by width, computed by adding the measurements of the two main side placements. These should total at least 1½ times the dimension of the container, depending on whether height or width is greater. Here the height is greater. [KLENDER]

Nine geranium blooms and at least three buds
Twelve sprays of annual candytuft

DIRECTIONS

1. Prepare receptacle and fasten to candlestick. (See Chapter 4 and photo on page 57.)

2. Select two ivy runners that curve out in opposite directions to make a right and a left side of the design. Cut 20 inches. Insert into Oasis at either side of candlestick to cascade down the sides. Place so leaves are on upper side of stem, not underneath.

3. For central line, choose a branch of ivy shaped like a crook. This will give necessary height and a graceful curving line to drape candlestick. (You can create the same effect by joining a short and a longer branch.) Top line should rise 4 inches above surface of Oasis, lower line should extend down 10 inches, making an overall

Steps 6 and 7. Center and side placements of candytuft form a mound outline. [KLENDER]

Steps 8 through 10. Completed Design. Geraniums and ivy contribute mass through the center to close gaps and point direction to horizontal lines. [KLENDER]

measurement of 14 inches. Face top line slightly to left of center as though it were the top half of an S.

4. Cut two reinforcing lines to 17 inches. Insert one at each side to follow first placements.

5. Select a companion branch curved up for right-of-center placement. Cut to 7 inches. Insert so tip stands directly above center of design.

6. Cut two sprays of candytuft, 7 or 8 inches long. Insert horizontally at each side above ivy sprays.

7. Graduate other sprays to lace through the design. Insert at angles on each side of center, placing some near top, others lower, so as to vary levels.

8. Cut geranium stems in 3- to 6-inch lengths. Place shortest at center front and projecting forward. Place longest at top pointing up, and others toward each side.

9. Fill in between flowers with sprigs of ivy. For accent, place one or two large single leaves low to one side of central geranium.

10. For an all-round effect, repeat design at back, beginning with step 4. If arrangement will be viewed only from the front, finish back with ivy and a few flowers.

SUBSTITUTE PLANTS:

For ivy: Cotoneaster (*C. salicifolia floccosa*), leucothoe
For candytuft: Dusty miller, pachysandra
For geranium: Marigolds, zinnias

HELPFUL HINTS FOR STANDARD DESIGNS

1. Cut Oasis to fit sides of container snugly, but let reach 1 to 2 inches above rim of container, distance depending on quantity and size of plant materials.

2. Position a container with three legs to show one leg directly in front.

3. When gathering plant materials, cut stems longer than you need them.

4. Place stems close together as possible on the holder, but do not crowd.

5. Set straight stalks at different angles to vary directions.

6. Cut stems in unequal lengths or insert those of the same length at different angles to avoid placements at the same height.

7. Avoid facing all flowers in the same direction.

8. To create depth, recess some flowers behind others.

9. Allow breathing space between flowers to prevent a packed look.

10. Taper forms at edges of a design.

11. Keep airy forms, small sizes, and pale shades at top and outer areas.

12. Group together flowers of same type to avoid scattered, spotty effect.

13. Group dark colors and heavy forms in lower central area.

14. Use flowers in different stages of development from bud to full bloom.

FLOWERS MAKE A HOME. *The arrangement has been coordinated in color, size, and style with the furnishings in this setting of the Federal period. Oval Room from Willow Brook, 1799, "Baltimore at the Turn of the Century." Baltimore Museum of Art.* [SUTER] *See page 11.*

DESIGN IS EVERYWHERE. *Household paraphernalia finds new artistic identity. Trivets, children's blocks, curtain-rod covers, and Bunsen-burner tripods in new relationships open your eyes to design potential in your surroundings.* [KLENDER] *See page 21.*

INTERIOR DESIGN. *The drapery fabric sets the color scheme and tone for a composition of minerals with varieties of dried palm and painted banksia.* [KLENDER] *See page 98.*

COLLECT MATERIALS SELECTIVELY. *A few kinds—gladiolus, lilies, and loquat—related in texture, harmonious in color, and varied in form are so simply composed you could hold the design in your hand. Rakuware pot by Paul Soldner.* [COPE] *See page 29.*

HEIRLOOM. *An antique Coalport jug—its elegance matched by the plant material—becomes the feature of an arrangement not its container.* [KLENDER] *See page 98.*

MADE FOR EACH OTHER. *A perfect association of accessories, which serve as containers, plant material—ti leaves, dessert spoons, bird-of-paradise, croton—and background create a show-stopper.* [KLENDER] *See page 100.*

COLOR CIRCLE

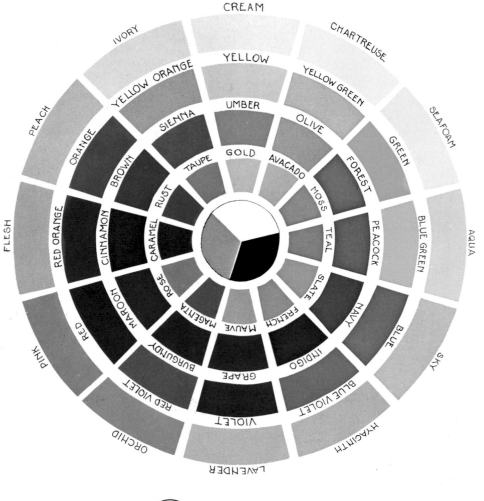

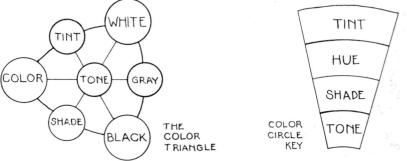

THE COLOR WHEEL. *Each color has been given an approximate name. The outer band: Tints, followed in order by hues, shades, and tones as circles decrease. The center: Neutrals—black, white, and gray—that mix with hues to make tints, shades, and tones. Lower left: Color triangle shows interaction of color and neutrals. Lower right: Key to interpret the chart. Artist, Mary F. Fitz-Patrick.* [SUTER] *See page 112.*

REVERENCE. *A Christmas arrangement in the three primary colors—red, blue, and yellow—set in the Saidie A. May Renaissance Room, Baltimore Museum of Art.* [SUTER] *See page 112, 119.*

RADIANCE. *An arrangement in analogous colors—yellow, yellow-orange, and orange. In a strict flower-show color class, the turquoise background and striped floor covering, not part of an analogous scheme, would disqualify this entry, as might conceivably the plum foliage. Black container is permissible.* [KLENDER] *See pages 113–115.*

GARDEN FAVORITES. *A candlestick container holds crested celosia, chrysanthemums, coleus, and prized ornamental cabbage, mostly in a monochromatic scheme of red-violet.* [KLENDER] *See page 115.*

COMPLEMENTS ATTRACT. *When integrated by color, very different materials—dried ivy vine, Plexiglas, and candle—seem less disparate. The shadow of the ivy behind the Plexiglas follows and merges with the design.* [SUTER] *See page 118.*

FROM FRESH TO DRIED. *The garden yields copper beech, celosia, and yarrow to dry, the roadside, heracleum or cow parsnips for long-lasting arrangements indoors.* [KLENDER] *See page 146.*

INFINITE VARIETY. *Graceful leucothoe glycerinized, air-dried celosia, yarrow, straw flowers, and commercially obtained golden mushrooms share common textures and have varied but related colors.* [SUTER] *See page 147.*

PROPPER IN PLACE. *Supported and held in place by a metal rod or wooden dowel sunk in a base, a root can stand on tiptoe indefinitely. A second rod is cemented to the shell, cupholders that supply moisture to the anthuriums.* [FITZ-PATRICK] *See page 161.*

REAL OR FAKE? *An authentic George III eighteenth-century epergne with fruit makes a permanent centerpiece if filled with fake edibles.* [FITZ-PATRICK] *See page 165.*

15. Buy in-bud stage and set some stalks in water in a warm place where flowers will open; keep others tight by storing in a cool place.

16. When using foliage branches as structural lines, place to show front not back of leaves.

17. Strip off all foliage that is below the water line.

18. Emphasize one color.

19. Use contrasts sparingly.

20. For a main line, avoid crotched branches that form a V at the top like rabbit ears.

21. Avoid placing flowers with heads downcast; position or wire them to tilt up. Flowers above rim of container look more graceful when curving down.

22. Avoid a "stunted" effect that results when height of arrangement equals the height of container.

23. If tip of foliage branch hangs too far forward, remove one or more leaves at the top to lighten the weight.

7

IMAGINATIVE ACCESSORIES

Combining accessories with flowers and foliage is an effective way to decorate your home. Although vases and bowls are generally used to display plant materials, figures or other ornaments can replace containers as focus for a design. When related by common characteristics and unified within a composition, an artistic object against a background of flowers and foliage makes an imaginative display that suggests a still-life painting.

Various kinds of accessories can be incorporated into a floral design, such as figures, lids from pots or other pieces of tableware, rocks, shells and minerals, boxes, books, photographs and paintings, implements, holiday ornaments, discards, metals, plastics, and pieces of bric-a-brac.

How to Use An accessory is defined in the National Council's "The Handbook of Flower Shows" as "A Component of an arrangement, or anything in the arrangement other than plant materials, background, container or base." Under this interpretation, even small stones that conceal mechanics are termed accessories. Candles are included except when they flank a table centerpiece. Then they become part of "the decorative unit," a standard feature of show tables. Although driftwood, fungi, and roots normally fit in the category of dried plant materials, in a flower show they are considered accessories if used in competitive classes requiring fresh flowers and foliage, and this applies to fresh fruit in a dried exhibit. However, in both instances, the nonconforming material, if permitted, must *not* be included in the arrangement itself but lie next to it as an auxiliary unit.

Select plant materials that are compatible with an accessory in form, color, size, and texture. Make sure all are related in character as well, suggesting the same style and origin. For example, if an African mask is the keynote, the design should feature strong colors and bold materials. Other factors influencing the choice of accessory might be a holiday or occasion, the season of the year, the decoration of a room, and the association of the accessory itself. For instance, flags in a *bon voyage* exhibit help to convey its purpose; gem stones carved as eggs add elegance to an Easter decoration. On the other hand, a delicate porcelain shepherdess and anthuriums, representing different locales, are not well related, nor is a Mexican plate a proper complement for a Victorian arrangement.

The shape of an accessory suggests the pattern of design that may either follow the lines of a figure or run counter to it. If the object is of heavy visual weight it will need taller plant material and more of it than if it is delicate. The size of an accessory determines proportion and scale; balance depends on its position. If the accessory faces forward, a symmetrical composition may look best; if it is turned sideways an off-center design may be indicated.

Placement　　An accessory may dominate a design or be placed in a subordinate position. If it is tall and imposing, it may tower above the plant material, and this results in the simplest and easiest design of all, requiring only a few flowers and sprays of foliage at the base for a triangular, crescent, or horizontal pattern. Such a design, however, is rarely acceptable in flower shows as the accessory rather than the plant materials is of paramount importance. In compositions more commonly seen in competition, a sparse line treatment makes a frame for a figure, or a mass of foliage and flowers, a background.

An accessory can also stand in a subordinate position beside the arrangement, instead of within it. Here the figure should be relatively smaller, no longer inspiring nor dictating the design. For example, a woodland composition of pine and daffodils might be augmented with a little animal figure or a nesting bird. A rosary draped beside a design of blackened branches and Easter lilies would accent rather than dominate the theme. In each case, the floral unit would be made in a separate holder or receptacle with the accessory placed apart.

Scale and Proportion

Scale is important when you use accessories. The object must appear in the same size ratio to the design as it would in reality. For example, animals do not dwarf trees nor is a shell equal in size to human figure. A deer resting beneath a tree would not be equal to one-half the size of the tree. To be in proper scale, a magnolia bloom would require a figure of different size from that proper for a violet. Sometimes, however, size exaggeration can be purposely used for emphasis. Man's helplessness in relation to the universe might be represented by contrasting a small figure with a big branch.

The color and quantity of flowers and foliage must also be related to the character of the accessory. A frail pale form would be lost among masses of bright flowers. When the accessory is the center of interest and substitutes for a container as well, it replaces the container as the standard for measuring proportion. The height of the accessory or width (whichever is greater) determines that of the plant materials, and this in turn demarcates the highest and widest limits of the design.

Following the standard practice of stem length in relation to container, the longest piece should measure from one-and-a-half, to two-and-a-half times the height of the accessory, depending on its visual weight. Large accessories require a taller design than small ones. Other flowers and foliage continuing the framework are then measured in relation to the principal stem.

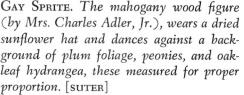

GAY SPRITE. *The mahogany wood figure (by Mrs. Charles Adler, Jr.), wears a dried sunflower hat and dances against a background of plum foliage, peonies, and oakleaf hydrangea, these measured for proper proportion.* [SUTER]

Bases and Holders

To develop a design that includes an accessory, first select a harmonious base on which to place the object, plant materials, and the mechanics to hold them. The base should be large enough to accommodate the whole composition but not overpower it. Dark bases look heavier than light-colored ones. Footed styles often need larger arrangements than simple flat ones. Compatibility of materials that compose the base and accessory is also important, as are the colors and textures. For example, if a figure is made of wood, a wooden base will probably associate best. But do not mix rough and highly polished finishes. If you take care to relate the base to the accessory, such ridiculous combinations as a china ballerina on a bamboo raft or a plastic sculpture on a marble slab will be avoided. Bases backed with felt prevent scratching furniture.

When an accessory instead of a container is used, a separate receptacle is needed to hold the arrangement and also to supply water for any fresh flowers and greens. Then a cupholder is ideal and these come in various shapes and sizes to accommodate a number of stems in a small space. A crescent type is often the most useful as it fits snugly beside any accessory that is rounded at the base. Made of heavy brass or iron, cupholders anchor the design firmly. Placed behind, or to the side of an accessory, the holder can, if necessary, be secured to the base with clay, but experiment first to determine the best direction for the design. When the arrangement is completed, add water and replenish it daily for the small amount in the holder evaporates overnight.

In Flower Shows   There are guidelines that regulate the use of accessories in flower shows. In competition, make sure the schedule permits an accessory in the class you are entering. No matter how much you may want to display it, don't attempt to camouflage or contrive its inclusion if the rules forbid it. I remember an entry in a class prohibiting accessories that incorporated a beautiful iridescent pink mineral placed in front to look as though it were the container for pink flowers. The mechanics in back had been so cleverly concealed with moss that it was almost impossible to discover where the edge of the rock terminated. The judges, however, were not fooled, and refused to give the design an award, although in other respects they agreed it deserved first place.

When it is subordinate to a design, an accessory must still contribute to it. There is a sound and time-honored phrase, "When in doubt, leave the accessory out." However, an accessory can perform the important function of interpreting a theme, or extending the line of a symmetrical design to give visual weight where balance is

SHY AND DEMURE. *Sheltered by sweet pepper bush and accented by rubrum lilies 'Jamboree,' both from the garden, a graceful figure, as the dominant interest, stands on two rounds of marble large enough to hold the arrangement as well. A crescent cupholder serves as container.* [SUTER]

needed. If you were entering a class "Nature Versus Industry," you might incorporate glass slag at the base of an arrangement featuring plant materials. A bit of coral, on the other hand, could continue the line of a curving piece of driftwood, if placed apart from it, off to the side. Facing toward each other and held on the same base, the two, even though separated, would be a unit. An accessory can also emphasize rhythm, add depth, and accent color or textural interest.

The more prominent the position of an accessory, the larger it will look in relation to the arrangement. A form placed at the back of a composition seems smaller because it is less conspicious than one in the foreground. A figure in profile appears less dominant

LAUREL IN SPRING. *Though it acts as container, the geode is definitely an accessory. It would disqualify an arrangement in a flower-show class where accessories were not permitted.* [SUTER]

than one facing forward. If an accessory looks too large, it can be partially concealed with plant material; this sometimes reduces the impression of size.

The accessory should appear in appropriate context. Fish do not belong in a desert scene, people don't stand in water unless dressed for such a situation, and butterflies are not identified with winter. The figure should be consistent in function with its normal role. A fan and sleigh bells do not associate, a mortar and pestle do not belong in an arrangement for a bedroom.

Selection In working with accessories, you will find simplicity a greater asset than excessive ornamentation. Clean lines, restrained color, a minimum of detail, and characteristics true to origin all reflect good taste. The number of accessories should be limited as profusion is unnecessary to convey a message and creates clutter as well. A library theme incorporating a book, eyeglasses, a quill, and an inkwell has been overstated. When used as auxiliary, the accessory should not compete for attention with the arrangement. It may be placed close to, or apart from, but it must not divide the composition into two equal parts. Carelessly placed accessories disturb logical organization and destroy fluidity.

In period designs, the accessory may be plant material lying apart from the floral unit. In medieval paintings, we see a sheaf of wheat placed beside a vase; in seventeenth- and eighteenth-century art fruits and flowers are strewn at the base of compositions. Accessories can suggest the characteristics of an era: a fan for rococo coquetry; a Corinthian column, the neoclassic revival; a grouping of apples the post-impressionistic forms of Cezanne.

Accessories—other than plant material—*incorporated* in an arrangement are not characteristic of early period designs. However, in Flemish interpretations, an insect or butterfly may be placed casually on a blossom. When you enter a period class in a flower

PRAYER. *Contributing but subordinate, two statutes of Buddha contribute to the theme, accent the design, and improve balance by extending the line of the lowest ti leaf.* [KLENDER]

show, consult an authentic painting to determine what accessories are appropriate.

In modern work, an accessory is important as art rather than for its realistic or narrative function. It contributes color, texture, pattern, or line, increasing their possibilities. Metals, scrap, plastics, and machinery can contribute form to an arrangement. In modern art, twisted tubing or a heap of crumpled wire has no identity as such and is, therefore, freed from conventional association. Thus the spectator can interpret according to his own experience.

In competition, any object other than container, base, background, and plant materials (except when lying apart) falls in the category of an accessory. A common error occurs when an accessory and an arrangement are inconsistent in scale. In most instances, exhibitors are likely to include a figure that is too large in comparison to the size of individual plant materials, to the container, or to the design as a whole. Therefore, when you choose an accessory, study the scale of the composition as a unit to make sure the relationships of the parts are sensible and sized according to their ratios in reality.

Still-life Designs

Still-life compositions (better suited to flower shows than house decoration) reverse the usual roles of accessory and arrangement. Normally, one accessory is adequate to interpret a theme and supplement design. But regardless of its importance, an accessory, even when the center of interest, should never dominate the plant material. However, in still-life classes, differentiated from "An Arrangement with Accessories," the opposite is true, the number and prominence of objects outweighing flowers and foliage. Here, several accessories are required because they are the chief means of relaying the theme. For example, if "The Garment Industry" were being interpreted, pieces of dress pattern, cloth, scissors, and other paraphernalia would be the main attraction and at the same time reveal the topic.

In a still-life, objects must also be life-size and true to function, not toys or miniatures. Thus, if figures of animals are being displayed, those naturally small, as birds or insects, could be included but not models of horses or dogs that would require reduction of normal size to fit in with a standard floral composition. Although correct scale must still be observed throughout, in a still-life the accessories should be of more significance than the arrangement.

8

MAKING THE MOST OF COLOR

How well do you cope with color? Can you match a scarf with a suit? Coordinate the furnishings of your home? Is your taste admired?

Color is a strong influence on our consciousness, following us continuously throughout our waking hours. It is so basic to our language that if we attempt to express the sensation of color with synonyms, none but the term itself conveys the image and meaning so clearly, so vividly. Color begins to haunt us at birth, establishing our identity by pigment of skin, eyes, and hair. As soon as we can identify what we see, color relationships begin to creep in. It is claimed that in the formative years, constant exposure to unpleasant shades at home, in school, or in other public places can produce personality problems and learning difficulties.

Color is an instrument in teaching. Children use paint to communicate thoughts and feelings. They recognize shapes by fitting blocks into holes of the same hue. A child begins to read by seeing his name above the blue hook where he hangs his coat.

Color can replace words to transmit information. Gray hair is a sign of age; rosy cheeks, bloodshot eyes indicate different states of health. Changes in color warn of food deterioration. Color can convey rage, excitement, despair. It indicates heat and cold as symbols of fire and ice. Color is an efficient yet easy method of relaying directions and messages—warning of danger, controlling movement, differentiating between opposing sides in sports or battle, and signifying defeat. To an artist, it is a tool for expressing ideas, attracting, focusing, or repelling attention.

Most of us approach color from a personal point of view with emphatic preferences and prejudices. Sometimes our attitudes reflect a childhood experience involving a favorite blue toy, or kissing a disagreeable relative who always wore pink. Words like vibrant, heavenly, and clear, or bilious, drab, and muddy imply reactions to shades.

In Flower Arrangement

Arranging flowers increases color perception. When you make a design, you test combinations to find the one that looks best. As in painting, you can emphasize a particular hue to create a mood. Color sets the tone of an arrangement as cheerful or somber, casual or formal, modern or traditional, delicate or dramatic. Although but one element of design, it influences all the others, defining line, form, and space, establishing pattern, and emphasizing textures. However, the purpose of color is to enhance design, not to substitute for it. Although various principles are affected by color, it is not fundamental to the basic design. But color exerts strong influence. If poorly chosen, it can ruin an otherwise good design, yet the impact of a dramatic palette can distract attention from deficiences in a composition. Test the effect of color on design by comparing an actual arrangement with a photograph of it in black and white. Faults previously camouflaged become noticeable.

Color and Design Principles

In selecting and composing plant materials, think of their color in relation to design principles as well as for their compatibility. For example, a dozen red roses by themselves in an arrangement would look monotonous because they are all alike. Yet, at the same time they would overstimulate the eye, saturating it with their intense chroma. Although it is true green leaves and stems provide some relief, the contrast is inadequate because it is scattered rather than concentrated. Grouping leaves would unify them, thereby increasing their effectiveness. However, the quantity would be small enough to preserve the dominance of red.

Conversely, too many different flowers disrupt unity. Some colors and forms must be repeated for rhythm and continuity. Furthermore, an excessively colorful design is almost impossible to integrate, whereas if colors are combined in equal amounts, a divided composition results. Although some contrast is needed, too much causes colors to compete for attention. Allowing one hue to predominate keeps variety under control. Observe nature's way of apportioning color in the landscape. Vast areas of cool blues and greens, restful to the eye, are accented with vivid flowers and birds that by contrast are of small size.

Through shade and intensity, color alters balance, proportion, and scale. Although dark and light flowers may be of equal number, they do not balance visually since dark and bright hues look heavier. Therefore, when you arrange, increase the quantity of pale flowers to compensate for the visual weight of deep shades. Color also influences top and bottom weight. When dark colors are placed above soft tints, a design will seem to fall under its own weight. For example, in a flower show, exhibitors were asked to make an arrangement suggesting the rainbow. The best composition from the standpoint of design and construction was, nevertheless, top-heavy, since colors were layered, deep purple iris at the top. In attempting to reproduce nature according to scientific theory, the contestant destroyed artistic balance, and so lost an award.

The placement of colors in an arrangement is really a simple matter of logic, if you distribute them in relation to their visual effect. Dark shades in the lower areas provide weight at the bottom where it is needed; bright colors that attract more attention should be featured in the center to create focus; while light hues that look airy belong at the top and edges to give lift to a design. This is an almost foolproof method for balancing color in traditional compositions, although modern design often breaks conventional rules for purposes of impact.

Color also plays tricks on proportion and scale. Contrary to expectation, dark colors that make flowers look heavier do not also enlarge their size; in fact, they make flowers look compact, shrinking size. Yet, the radiating quality of bright blossoms seems to magnify their size. Of all colors, yellow looks largest, white and red follow. In a situation where flowers are already unequal in size and scale, color differences can make matters worse.

The Color Wheel You will find it easier to select and coordinate colors if you are familiar with harmonies on a color wheel. Of the various theories of color, the pigment theory is the most appropriate for flower arrangement because it divides the color circle almost evenly between warm and cool hues. The wheel is composed of three triangles. The first includes the three primary colors—red, blue, and yellow— so-called because they are the source of all colors and cannot be produced by combining other colors. Each hue, mixed equally with the next, makes secondary colors; red and yellow for orange, yellow and blue to make green, and blue and red to get violet. These six, known as spectrum hues, provide the ingredients for a third set known as tertiary or intermediate colors. Named for their parents, they are blue-green, blue-violet, red-violet, red-orange, yellow-orange, and yellow-green. Thus, by their composition and proximity, the twelve hues comprise color harmonies.

Adjacent colors make up related harmonies: those opposite, contrasting schemes. Because of their aggressive qualities, red, yellow, and orange are warm and advancing; blue, green, and violet, are cool, receding hues. Seen on a wheel, these harmonies further demonstrate how the distance between colors alters their intensity. Bright colors side by side look duller than when paired with their opposites. For example, orange doesn't seem nearly as vivid next to yellow as it does beside blue whose opposite chroma increases contrast.

Analogous Colors

By referring to standard schemes in selecting colors, you can avoid errors and at the same time improve your color sense. Simply choose the combinations you like best or those appropriate for the purpose, and use them as a basis for creating your own harmonies. For example, since you know that blue and orange contrast, but their effect together is not exactly what you want, you might try pairing their relatives, aqua and coral.

Analogous colors are probably the most popular of all harmonies due to their rhythmic flow of color and their familiar associations. For instance, a composition in purple, green, and blue could recall a scene of mountains and valley against the sky, while yellow, yellow-orange, and red-orange might suggest a roaring fire. Because they share characteristics, analogous colors are more easily reconciled by the eye than complementary ones with their sharp differences. Since it is true that some combinations of related hues are more stimulating than others—such as yellow, orange, and red as opposed to red, red-violet, and violet—intensity is, nevertheless, weakened when colors change gradually. Analogous harmonies, therefore, usually appeal to conservative tastes.

Color Schemes in Competition

Although it is not necessary to follow rules in making analogous arrangements for your home, you must conform to requirements in flower shows. Here any number of adjacent colors are permitted but although the range is limited to one primary and one-third of the color wheel, the scheme must include at least three hues. However, exact harmonies are more useful as a guide to color organization than as competitive classes in which exhibitors must match perfectly colors in an arrangement to a corresponding harmony on a printed color wheel. Finding flowers and foliage in the exact shades as manufactured hues can be an impossible task. Although formerly a standard category in flower shows, such regimented schemes have been outmoded.

Practical problems and confusion have been responsible for the change in attitude. In the first instance, plant materials do not grow in the same gradations of color as can be mixed with paints. Thus their hues do not fall into a rigid sequence. Furthermore, fresh flowers of certain color are not always obtainable because they are out of season, native to some other climate, or a nonexistent variety. To illustrate, it is impossible in winter to find lilacs for an arrangement keyed to violet; if blue spikes are required, delphinium are not reliably hardy in hot, dry climates; the red Fuji chrysanthemum, if wanted for a strong center of interest, has yet to be hybridized; turquoise materials, with the exception of ampelopsis (better known as turquoise berry-vine), have almost no source, eliminating turquoise entirely; and grayed flowers are indeed rare.

Besides these difficulties, exhibitors were continually making errors in choosing materials of the right color, especially for analogous schemes. For example, if an arrangement is composed of oranges and yellows, the incorporation of green foliage from plants other than those included in the design would be outside the scope of the harmony, thereby disqualifying the entry. Thus, an arrangement that contained peony leaves with tritoma, celosia, and zinnias all in shades of yellow, yellow-orange, and orange would be eliminated because green would not be a part of the scheme and peony leaves would not be the natural foliage of any of the flowers. However, their own leaves would be permitted. The same fate would befall an arrangement with a base, background or container of the wrong hue. Any of these displaying in total, or in part even a minuscule spot of color foreign to the scheme would be grounds for labeling the exhibit, "Not In Competition." Even so, neutrals have always been permitted, provided they are subordinate.

It has been customary for judges of analogous color classes to check comformance with an actual color wheel to make certain that the scheme of plant materials did not cross boundaries into another range or disrupt the sequence. For example, orange-red flowers must occupy a middle position between orange and red ones, not following or preceding them. Blooms with yellow centers or variegated leaves are another pitfall, yellow being unacceptable unless it is within the designated harmony. Many a blue ribbon has been lost by those who failed to understand and, consequently, did not observe to the letter, the severe limitations of color schemes. Flower shows now emphasize the *creative* use of color to interpret moods, occasions, or characteristics, such as youth or festiveness. Sometimes color classes are purely decorative, requiring a design keyed to a particular hue.

Monochromatic Harmony

Monochromatic harmony is another kind of related scheme similar to analogous but different because it encompasses the full range of only one color. A color can be modified by adding white, black, or gray. The composition of a monochromatic harmony is better understood when color is considered in terms of its dimensions or qualities as hue, value, and chroma.

Hue is the name of a color as red or blue.

Value indicates lightness or darkness, and is composed of tints or shades made by mixing a hue with white, or black, respectively. Thus, black and blue would create the shade of navy; white with violet, the tint lavender.

Chroma refers to intensity that can be graded by the amount of gray added, resulting in tones. When we speak of toning down a color, we reduce its intensity. Rose is an example of the tone made from red and gray. Therefore, a monochromatic harmony in red could include any of its many tints, tones, and shades—pink, rose, maroon, etc., as well as red, itself. The process of combining color and neutral is best illustrated by a color triangle developed for this purpose by the noted color authority, Faber Birren.

Because of the many degrees in variation of a color, it is difficult to describe unusual shades. A term like peacock-blue does not indicate the exact composition of this color, which could have different meanings for different people. To solve the problem, Alfred Munsell devised a system of Color Notation, a mathematical formula to describe color, providing nomenclature as well. The code Hv/c represents the color name first, followed by the degree of weakness or strength of its value and intensity. The scale ranges from 0 for the darkest and grayest to 10 for white, and even higher for full chroma. Thus R5/5 would describe a medium red because both numbers are midway between the highest and lowest value and chroma.

A monochromatic scheme includes plant materials restricted in color to tints, tones, and shades of the chosen hue. Black, white, and gray are also permitted. Although this harmony is probably the most restrained of all, it need not be uninteresting. Contrasts of light and dark offer one way of dramatizing monochromatic schemes; variations in textures and forms, another. Dried arrangements in mellow tans and browns, or all-foliage designs in gradations of green are prime examples of the pleasing effects possible with single-color harmonies. In the home they serve to unify colorful furnishings or provide relief from intense hues nearby.

Neutrals   In flower arrangement, neutrals are considered to be colors, although scientifically, black is the absence of color; white the presence of all colors. But, since black and white produce unique sensations different from those of pure color, and also alter the character of hues, the arranger sees them as colors.

Since neutrals in a colorful design can improve or disturb it, try to evaluate their influence when you first plan an arrangement. Black makes a forceful background for pale and bright colors, increasing their intensity. Repeated as accent, dried leaves painted black, help to unify divergent hues and also create rhythm. Illustrations of the effectiveness of recurring black can be seen in the paintings of Rouault, who created a stained-glass quality in his compositions by employing black throughout to separate, emphasize and integrate patches of different colors. Although a black base can help to anchor an arrangement visually, if it is massive, it can also have a bottom-heavy effect. Black containers contribute drama to a black-and-white design, provide relief from vivid colors, but usually overpower pastel flowers, sharply dividing such a composition into independent parts.

White adapts well to traditional or modern designs. But a white container holding colorful plant materials will compete with them for attention, disrupting unity by splitting the design. On the other hand, a white vase or bowl combines suitably with all white or partly white flowers and foliage like that of rubrum lilies and caladiums or with plants of a whitish cast, such as dusty miller, mullein, or lamb's-ears (*Stachys*). Since white flowers are not entirely white, incorporating green or yellow-green stems and foliage, the natural affinity of these colors makes them compatible in a white container provided they are combined in proper proportions.

Because white has less visual weight than either yellow or green, these two would look best in smaller amounts placed centrally. Greater quantities of white would balance them and at the same time dominate the design, thus unifying instead of dividing it.

Variegated leaves add interest to a design and, if needed, small, light green foliage can form part of the outline to soften edges. If an arrangement is massive, shades of orange, used sparingly in close groupings, might also be included. A traditional composition might include white snapdragons, yellow and white roses, pale orange chrysanthemums, white Easter and orange Mid-Century lilies with variegated leucothoe and aucuba in a white alabaster urn on a white marble base.

For a modern interior, a sparse arrangement of a few bold white flowers, or smaller ones tightly bunched (to give them the appearance of a larger form), and dried foliage painted black could make a dramatic contribution to surroundings in solid colors, or patterned furnishings in a neutral scheme. However, as a background, white gives insufficient contrast to an all-white arrangement, and is unsatisfactory behind a colorful design because then contrast is too extreme. White usually creates a harsh outline, in addition to glare, and is likely to produce shadows that distort a design. In flower shows, it is rare for exhibits to be staged on white table coverings since these are a disturbing element.

In antithesis to black and white, gray is completely versatile. It enhances almost any color because of its wide range in value. A vase tinted soft gray has a delicate quality similar to that of pastel flowers, while a deeper gray vase bears close relationship to blooms darker in hue. Gray can also have a decidely warm or cool cast if red or blue is part of its composition. Therefore, a container or background can be painted a shade of gray corresponding in tone to the scheme of the design by the addition of the main color to the mixture, or by brushing the main hue lightly over the surface. If an all-gray arrangement, as one of driftwood or painted materials, lacks sparkle, its neutral quality could make almost any other color companionable without discord.

Contrasting Colors Complementary schemes combine anywhere from two to four colors. The simplest, the direct complement, is composed of two colors directly across on the circle, such as red and green. These harmonies are by nature more dynamic and forceful than related harmonies. In a contrast of warm against cool (primary against secondary), each intensifies the strength of the other. As the name implies, one completes the other, the secondary color embodying the qualities of the other two primaries. For example, orange completes blue as it is actually part red, part yellow. Purple and yellow create a scheme that is a variation of yellow, red, and blue. Complementary schemes can also be made from tertiary colors, such as yellow-green with red-violet, or blue-green and red-orange, as well as from any tints, tones, or shades of any hues lying opposite.

Because they are so totally different in character, colors in a contrasting scheme tend to pull apart if they are not unified by the dominance of one of them. An arrangement in complementary colors might incorporate a few orange gerberas with salvia and delphinium in light and dark shades of blue in a blue-gray container. Here, a black base could strengthen unity. A poorly co-ordinated scheme might alternate a blue base, an orange container, blue hydrangeas in the center, against a background of orange gladiolus interspersed with cornflowers and blue echinops. The striped effect would separate the design into layers that could be avoided if either orange or blue created a continuing path through the composition.

For those who find direct complements too extreme, split complements produce a milder effect while retaining the character of opposites. Composed of three rather than two colors, split complements (as the name implies) combine one hue with each of those on either side of the direct complement. Thus, blue would skip orange and team instead with yellow-orange and red-orange, moderating the sharp differences. These schemes are most successful when only one primary or secondary color is included, the other two drawn from the tertiary family. Therefore, avoid a mixture like blue-violet with orange and yellow as the two intense warm hues would overpower the cooler one.

Triads comprise three hues that span the color wheel at equidistant points. These harmonies are composed of all primaries, all secondaries, or all tertiaries. Combined at full strength, they would be difficult to unify as each has a distinct personality. Varying them in value brings them under control. You have only to think of the lovely pastel quality of French eighteenth-century styles that feature pink, pale blue, and gold. In pure form, they make the primary triad, red, blue and yellow.

Paired Complements or Tetrads

Paired complements or tetrads are composed of four hues, including two pairs on the wheel at equidistant points. Dividing them between high and low values gives the best effect, although in general other types of harmonies are better suited to floral design.

Beware of Orange

A word of caution on the use of orange. Orange has a very loud voice. The combination of just one citrus orange or kumquat with any fruits, vegetables, or flowers in other colors is impossible to subdue. Orange china, place mats, or napkins, if excessively bright can make a table setting spotty. Even the small quantities of orange in the bird-of-paradise flower have a glaring and hard quality. Studies show that orange is one of the least liked colors (along with purple). Improper or too liberal use of it in flower show competition may result in the loss of an award, as many judges feel it has a tendency to dominate all other elements. However, it is especially suited to modern arrangements; in traditional compositions orange seems less offensive when tempered with related gold, woody browns, and red-orange, a harmony so typical of fall.

Importance of Background Color

When a home arrangement is made, the color of the walls influences the scheme of flowers and foliage. In flower shows, the floral design is generally completed first, the background chosen afterwards. Then various colored fabrics or poster boards can be tried behind it to see which looks best. It is surprising how colors are altered by different backdrops; some ruin a design, while perhaps only one or two enhance it. I have found in experimenting with background colors my last choice sometimes proves best, whereas the hue I thought most promising did not live up to expectations.

Since surrounding colors influence human behavior and efficiency, studies have been made to determine schemes best suited to hospitals, stores, and factories. Findings in these areas can be helpful to flower arranging. For example, the reaction to color of patients suffering from emotional disturbances is contrary to popular belief. According to psychiatric tests, bright surroundings instead of cheering depressed patients tend to intensify meloncholia, the warm shades contrasting too sharply with despondency. Nor do receding tones quiet hyperactive types, who seem to react best to the strong chromas consistent with their character. Colors, therefore, can be identified with personalities, those who like advancing hues are likely to be aggressive; introverts are reputedly fond of blues and greens. Consequently, if a flower show class is entitled "Agitation," the exhibitor would know to use a bright background with flowers of intense colors.

One color expert studied the effects of color in operating rooms. It was once customary to paint walls white to create optimum visibility and an atmosphere of cleanliness, but the theory was not substantiated in practice. Under the strong lights required for surgery, white caused a glare that produced eye strain. Blue-green was then recommended because it complements the color of blood and the human complexion, and also softens glare thus reducing fatigue. In applying medical findings to flower arrangement, I discovered pale aqua or turquoise makes a perfect background for almost any flowers.

Success in business might be contingent on the color selected as a setting for transactions. Merchandise displayed against an unpopular shade and products packaged without regard for color appeal can ruin sales. In a restaurant or beauty shop, colors or lights that cast a green shadow repel customers. The color of packaging could promote sales of a supermarket item to a greater degree than the contents of the can, depending on whether the consumer prefers tomatoes pictured against blue or yellow. Differences in taste among buyers must be considered in correlating colors with markets. In the past, merchandise aimed at lower-income groups sold better if designed in standard schemes; in high-income brackets, prospects were greater for products in unusual shades. Now, with significant purchasing power in the hands of young people, wilder combinations are becoming routine.

When a flower show schedule requires the interpretation of a theme, color becomes a language. We are familiar with moods suggested by color—yellow for cowardice, caution, and ill-health; green for freshness or envy; black to symbolize dishonor, grief, and death, and many others. Translated into flowers and foliage, color becomes the medium of a message, and is so crucial in competition that a superior design can forfeit first place if the color interpretation is not right. Here are some examples. To suggest winter, snapdragons, lilies, roses, and spiraea, even though white, would not compose an arrangement typical of the season because they grow in summer. In a class, "Air Pollution," an entry of green foliage against a gray background, no matter how expertly arranged, might not win if it gave an impression of life and growth at dusk, rather than the intended one of stagnation. An arrangement portraying "Physical Fitness" in shades of yellow for sunshine could also receive a low score if the judges associated yellow with the pallor of ill-heath. Even though an exhibitor tried to be original by representing "Spring Fever" with white flowers, mirrors, and clear plastic to symbolize fluffy clouds and rain, judges might think these characteristics conveyed snow and ice, preferring instead a design in hot pinks and oranges that intensified spring shades. Thus, one hue may have several connotations, depending on the context in which it is used and the observer's reaction. When you plan a scheme for an arrangement, especially in a flower show, consider the implications from various points of view.

Create Your Own With colors already organized into so many harmonies, there would seem to be little opportunity for originating new ones. Yet there are popular combinations for which no definite category exists. For example, the scheme red, white, and blue, signifying patriotism, has universal appeal, partly perhaps, because red and blue are the best liked of any colors. Pink and orange, or green and blue might be remembered from the past when they were promoted in furnishings and fashions. Don't hesitate to try unorthodox color combinations for fear of being labeled "way out." Applying the principles of color harmony will better equip you to experiment.

9

MINIATURES ARE FUN

Place a miniature flower arrangement on a table in the living room and it immediately captures attention, although it may not be more than eight inches high. Small things fascinate both young and old. The perfection of a tiny plant that grows and matures like a large one is a source of wonder. An ornament sized to fit a dollhouse credits the craftsman with skill and patience. Thus miniature arrangements may arouse greater interest than full-sized ones, perhaps because a little design looks more intricate.

Bits and pieces, scraps and snippings, young and dwarf growth are the ingredients of miniatures. Consequently they do not require much time, work or money, or even space to display. Appealing to many ages and situations, a small arrangement can occupy invalids or amuse children. Tiny bouquets look as attractive on a sickroom tray as they do on a party table, make an appropriate gift, and are saleable for fund raising.

Types of Containers — The search for small containers is a hobby in itself. Centuries ago the aristocracy in various countries began collecting valuable trinkets as presents or souvenirs. Such tokens as patchboxes, the famous Chelsea "toys," tiny figurines and other objects were created by artists in porcelain, enamel, ivory, jade, gold, and wood. Style and decoration reflect the taste of yesterday. More functional but of

TINY TOTS. *On two levels in two heights, an antique cloisonné vase, no more than 4 inches high, holding a twig and a spray of tiny roses, is complemented by a brass incense burner 1½ inches tall, containing a sprig of heather and some dwarf zinnias.* [SUTER]

MUTT AND JEFF. *A snip of cut-leaf dwarf Japanese maple and sedum pinched from a flower border are enough to fill two stoneware pots measuring no more than 4½ inches.* [SUTER]

WATCH SCALE. *The greatest pitfall in miniature arrangements is scale. Be sure materials are of consistent size. Here all are equally small in relation to containers. The door key sets the scale.* [SUTER]

equal merit were the miniatures made in china factories as workmen's models. Small editions of large pieces, they provided patterns for full-sized molds or were used as salesmen's samples. In addition to antiques, the category of traditional miniature vases and bowls includes many kinds of reproductions made to gratify the mania for collecting small things.

The acquisition of miniature containers is limited only by pocketbook or imagination. The affluent can choose vases, baskets, and urns from among such famous makers as Tiffany, Wedgwood, or Fabergé. Those of modest means may select from a wide range of household objects. Lipstick tubes, pillboxes and bottles, perfume vials, spice tins, egg cups, open salt dishes, toothpick and stamp holders, cordial glasses, matchboxes and jar lids can be converted into containers with paint or a covering of adhesive-backed paper. Not to be overlooked either is an adhesive tape ring with its cover. It becomes a well for flowers by adding a bottom to the opening in the center. Tops of tin cans also make odd-shaped containers if the edges are bent up with pliers to a depth that will hold water.

Even a bar of soap makes a receptacle for an arrangement. Suggesting fine minerals or gemstones in its new role, a container made of white soap looks like marble. Pink soap looks like quartz; green imitates jade. Carve it into an interesting shape and hollow out the center. If you seal the cavity with paraffin it will hold water.

Nature, too, provides an almost limitless supply of decorative holders. Bits of driftwood, stones, shells, coral, and pods are fine for either fresh or dried plant materials. Many have ready-made openings. Others can be sculptured to suit the arrangement.

Bases and Accessories

Use your imagination to see miniature bases in various useful objects. Consider buttons, pocket mirrors, boxtops, erasers, or sponges. Even the discs from a game of checkers are adaptable. And, you can make a base from wood, slate, glass, tile, cork, or fabric.

Tiny accessories are fun to incorporate into small arrangements. Toy counters and gift shops provide tiny animals, figures, kitchenware, fans, and frames. For modern design, have a look in hardware and dime stores for wire, nuts and bolts, screening, and scraps of tubing.

Mechanics and Tools

Like a full-sized flower arrangement, a small one needs a mechanic to hold plant materials in place. Tiny versions of needle-holders can be bought. A bit of Oasis can be wedged into a petite vase or urn with a wide opening, and substitutes can be made from "raw materials" found in most kitchens. Stuff a miniature tall container with toothpicks (cut to the height needed), leaving a shallow cavity at the top. Don't pack too tight—there will not be space enough to insert stems. Unpainted wooden toothpicks expand when wet and are better than plastic ones for holding materials in position.

Placed at the top, a bit of steel wool (not a soap pad), matted loosely, provides support for frail stems, and it may be sprayed in a color to match the design. If dried plant materials alone are arranged in a tall container, fill it with sand, Kitty Litter, or dry Oasis. A copper pot cleaner cut to size can also serve as a mechanic. If the opening of a vase is small, flowers and foliage can often support each other without an extra aid.

In a bowl, compote, or other shapes with a wide mouth, a needle-holder is usually best. But you can experiment with substitutes. For example, a small toothbrush is rather like a commercial holder. Saw off the handle and fasten the brush to the bowl with floral clay. As with tall containers, cover the bristles with steel wool to support soft stems. If very tender, wire them to twigs for reinforcement.

Small arrangements need frequent watering to keep them fresh. Hardening plant materials before arranging prolongs life. Tiny flowers and leaves like their large counterparts last longer if cut either early or late in the day. Submerge foliage in tepid water for several hours. Flowers respond to a long water bath with only their heads above the surface. Misting the arrangement helps keep it alive.

Special tools aid in constructing miniatures. A standard flower clippers is adequate for gathering plant materials, but, a small sewing or manicure scissors is handier for intricate trimming. Tweezers are usually better than fingers for inserting thin stems into tiny openings. Instead of a watering can, use an eye-dropper. A cake tester will pierce holes in Oasis for materials with weak stems. Fine wire helps to support stems and shape them into curves and angles and is useful for fastening several together. A magnifying glass is often helpful.

Size and Scale   In the past, miniature arrangements in National Council Flower Shows were limited to five inches in height or width. Now they are called small arrangements, since size restriction has been increased to eight inches. Although helpful as a guide, these measurements need only be adhered to in competition.

Scale is most important in choosing materials for little designs. The size of the container determines the height and width of the arrangement, as well as that of blooms and leaves. As a rule, an arrangement should be almost twice as tall or wide as the vase or bowl, the largest flower not more than one-third the size of the container.

When selecting materials, have the container at hand to compare sizes. A leaf that by itself looks small might be too large for the vase. Inconsistency in scale is quickly noticed when the two are together. Also, all parts of a plant may not be suitable. For example, a rosebud could be just right for a miniature but the leaves might be too large. When this occurs, remove the over-sized growth. When photographed, a properly scaled miniature arrangement appears full sized.

A Little Seems Like a Lot. *This mass design, though only 5 by 8 inches, without a standard for comparison looks to be full-size.* [SUTER]

NOT MUCH. *A few tiny pine cones and "feathers" from bird-of-paradise flowers are enough to fill a baby shell; a bit of fern, some chrysanthemum buds, and an end of podocarpus suffice for this diminutive modern Japanese container.* [SUTER]

LADY OF THE HOUSE. *She is a doll; the container, a tiny antique agate ash tray, is enhanced more by a design of Harry Lauder's Walking Stick and star flowers than by cigarette butts.* [HARRIS]

Suitable Plant
Materials

Hunting for small flowers and foliage will focus your attention on plant growth you may not have noticed before. You see buds and berries, terminal shoots of branches, tendrils of vines, burrs, pods and cones in new perspective. The list of suitable materials is long and includes acacia, acorn, ageratum, baby's breath, boxwood, buttercups, cacti, callicarpa, dill, ferns, feverfew, grape hyacinths, grasses, heath and heather, holly berries, lily-of-the-valley, myrtle, needled evergreens, parsley, privet berries, Scotch broom, spiraea, statice, strawflowers, succulents, violets, weeds and wildflowers. Large blossoms formed of many florets, such as delphinium, hydrangea or yarrow, can be cut into small sections that look like tiny single flowers.

Dwarf varieties of garden flowers, such as button chrysanthemums, geraniums, marigolds, roses, and zinnias are also good sources, as are snippings from house plants like begonias and wandering jew, as well as many others. The centers of daisy-type flowers, sticks and twigs (for line), and driftwood are other possibilities.

Only a small amount of material is needed for a miniature arrangement. Crowding destroys daintiness and excess obscures detail.

10

ARRANGEMENTS IN LINE

Bare branches found outdoors can become line arrangements indoors. Cut while still fresh branches from deciduous trees and shrubs dry in their dormant state to provide material that can be used year after year. Observe the natural pattern of leafless branches. These often suggest linear compositions that can be made for display inside on a chest or table. Perhaps you already have an eye for line without realizing it. If you like to sit by the fire and watch the flames disappear into smoke, throw pebbles into a pond to make ripples in the water, or watch a shapely figure walking down the street, you are already conscious of line.

In Nature   Line is popularly defined as a straight vertical or horizontal stroke drawn with a writing instrument. Simple linear shapes are encountered daily in the form of telephone poles, fences, lanes dividing traffic, and lamp posts. All are so commonplace that they are scarcely noticed.

Compared to these functional straight lines that have been manufactured by man are the natural ones of plants. Irregular, infinite in variety, they curve, twist, fork, cascade, radiate, cross, angle, or protrude in many directions. The interaction of these lines within a tree or shrub creates the design of the structure. A plant with excessive growth has a more complex pattern than one that is sparse. An

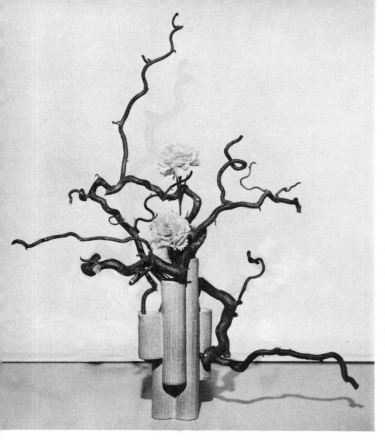

CROOKED AND TWISTING. *When properly pruned to feature the best lines, Harry Lauder's Walking Stick seems to dance around the modern container. Once constructed, the design lasts almost forever and can be easily varied by replacing fake carnations with other flowers.* [DIPAOLA]

image is compounded when several overgrown trees or shrubs are seen together. Then a jungle of interfering lines is produced that prevents each specimen from displaying an attractive appearance and the group from presenting a unified effect.

Hunting through a maze of branches to find the best shape and then visually blocking out the conflicting lines helps the eye to see pleasing patterns that can be used in arrangements. We all have noticed a lone tree that had apparently been struck by lightning. With only the strongest branches remaining, the structure of clean forceful lines made a memorable impression. Such a natural design has inspired artists and is an excellent model for the floral designer.

To Employ Line   In flower arranging, a few strong lines make a better design than many weak ones. It is also easier to construct. If branches are pruned to frame irregular spaces, the composition will benefit from

STRONG BRANCHES. *Dried manzanita and fresh Magnolia virginiana blossoms make a well-defined pattern. The pot, suggesting fungus growth, by Pauline Wright; the base, petrified wood.* [SUTER]

LINES OF MOVEMENT. *Just three lines and three leaf rosettes of photinia make a quick, simple design.* [KLENDER]

the contrast of lines and voids and an imposing silhouette will replace clutter. Furthermore, if many branches with many different directions are included, the viewer is discouraged because the eye cannot find a path through the tangle. When a few lines of a consistent direction are used, a composition appears organized and invites more prolonged inspection.

The simplest designs are composed of strong branches. A heavy line is more likely to hold attention because it creates a well-defined pattern against a wall or in space, and looks sturdy enough to stand independently without aid from auxiliary stems. Thus, one strong, well-shaped branch is likely to have sufficient structural form to make a complete arrangement. Old growth is preferable to new, as tender shoots or suckers are not sufficiently hardened and are likely to wilt.

When you employ frail, thin lines, more will be needed to construct a firm framework and arranging will be more difficult. One wispy stem is inadequate for a complete design or a substantial outline. Consider the bare branches of a flowering crab apple. One section of a limb is likely to be massive enough for an entire arrangement requiring only a large flower or two for color and accent. On the other hand, a single stem of pussy willow could not perform the same task due to its delicate lightweight structure. With this type of material, you will need five to seven branches for an arrangement.

Line expresses movement. Creating a path for the eye to follow, the tempo of a line influences the mood of a design and consequently the reaction of the viewer. Graceful curves are relaxing. Broken lines that change abruptly or zigzag are exciting as they cause the eye to move rapidly with little time to adjust to new directions.

Linear Materials   Trees and shrubs can be found whose growth patterns express either curvilinear or contorted rhythms. If you prefer a graceful cascade, weeping willow or cherry is as picturesque without leaves as with them. Reflected in water, one pendulous branch from either tree and a beautiful rock placed in a container create a scene that is restful and eye-appealing as well.

Many flowering trees and shrubs—the dogwood, tree lilac, star magnolia, pear, and quince—have well-shaped bare branches suitable for winter arrangements. Examine the whole plant critically, following the path of each limb until the most artistic bends and turns catch your eye. Then remove them for display indoors.

Harry Lauder's Walking Stick is a favorite for its twisted, gnarled stems that always attract attention. The trifoliate orange is also popular, although its nasty thorns may deter all but the most dedicated arrangers. Worth considering for graceful line are cotoneaster, witch-hazel, and the related corylopsis or winterhazel. Trees in the maple family are also a good source. If you have a long tree pruner,

NATURAL DESIGN. *The patterns of leafless winged euonymus branches are designs in themselves. Artificial roses add color and accent in an arrangement with permanence.* [DIPAOLA]

beech, horse chestnut, oak, sycamore, tulip-poplar or plane-tree will yield large decorative branches.

Two of the best specimens for textural interest are *Euonymus alatus* and sweetgum, the branches and twigs of both having corky bark. Their angular growth patterns and pliable stems can be bent to improve their natural lines. Willows offer distinctive characteristics. The upright French pussy willow is grown primarily for its soft furry catkins. Its appearance in flower shops while the weather is still blustery is a harbinger of spring. The contorted corkscrew or tortuosa and fantail willows are also favored for floral designs and can be found growing in many an arranger's garden.

Although the logical place to seek bare branches is on trees, many a useful stray limb can be found along the road blown there in a storm. Sometimes you will see professionals trimming or removing trees along a route of travel, and with luck retrieve from them a shapely branch before it is consigned to the grinder. Dumps, too, are often rewarding. Concealed in the debris, you may find a bough with a lovely flowing line exactly suited to your purpose. Scavenging can be profitable as well as fun.

Branches of both native and exotic trees can be found in floral shops. Of special interest are materials not hardy in all sections of the country. Dried manzanita wood from the West Coast is stocked by many florists, and this is prized for its curving and twisted lines. Available in tan or gray that results from sand-blasting, it is sometimes called ghost-wood because of its strange configuration. Edgeworthia, also known as mitsumata, has an interesting forklike branch popular with the Sogetsu School of Japanese flower arrangement.

11

DESIGNS WITHOUT FLOWERS

Attractive arrangements can be made without flowers. Broad-leaved and needle evergreens and indoor plants are fine sources of material for decorative designs. All-green arrangements are easily constructed by combining foliage branches with large bold leaves of varied form, pattern, color, and texture. You can explore the possibilities as you walk or drive, when you visit a nursery, or stroll through your own garden. And do have in mind the possibilities of all-foliage arrangements when you buy plants for your garden or winter windowsill.

Types of Foliage   You may be surprised at the different outlines of leaves. John Ruskin noticed that, "Leaves take all kinds of strange shapes as if to invite us to examine them." For example, anthurium is heart-shaped, rex begonia 'Black Knight' resembles a star, eucalyptus a coin; fatsia is scalloped, the Boston fern 'Fluffy Ruffles,' is lacy, holly serrated, ivy lobed, laurel oval, leucothoe lance-shaped, monstera perforated, palm fanlike, 'Emerald Ripple' peperomia corrugated, philodendron like an arrow, yucca a dagger. Contrasts can be created by combining these different forms.

In nature branches curve, twist, or cut through space at acute angles. Notice the undulating lines of Atlas cedar, leucothoe, pine, and rhododendron. Look for the natural curves of azalea, camellia, and laurel. Prune branches to reveal their graceful features or

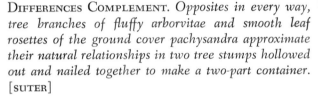

DIFFERENCES COMPLEMENT. *Opposites in every way, tree branches of fluffy arborvitae and smooth leaf rosettes of the ground cover pachysandra approximate their natural relationships in two tree stumps hollowed out and nailed together to make a two-part container.* [SUTER]

bend them by wiring or with gentle hand pressure. Notice that *Ilex convexa* forks sharply rather like the zigzagging pyracantha and *Berberis julianae,* both of which have dangerous thorns. Wear heavy gloves when working with these.

Ivy, philodendron, and wandering Jew produce green cascades. Juniper, ligustrum, and leatherleaf viburnum grow upright. Some shrubs—mahonia, nandina, and umbrella pine—radiate at the top like the spokes of a wheel. They are somewhat difficult to work with but effective when properly pruned.

FROM HOUSE PLANTS. *Bold lines of variegated aspidistra fall in graceful curves, framing monstera leaves as a center of interest in an oriental basket.* [SUTER]

Shape Determines Composition

The contour of branches often determines the form of an arrangement. Branches that grow straight are well suited to vertical, horizontal, or triangular designs. Crescent, oval, S-curve, or simple line designs require rhythmic material. For abstract or modern work, an angular silhouette is best. Radiating branches are appropriate for Japanese or contemporary styles. If you experiment with different combinations, you are likely to produce unusual designs. For example, a curved stem of leatherleaf viburnum in front of a vertical branch of yew becomes a green study of opposing directions and contrasting forms; a short-stemmed circle of mahonia creates a focus for a sweeping curve of red pine. Sprays of ligustrum at the back frame low clusters of golden arborvitae in front to hold the eye.

Foliage in Many Colors

Not all foliage is green. Therefore leaf color can play an important role in arrangements without flowers. Besides nuances of green, leaves have yellow, blue, purple, brown, silver, black, gray, and red shadings. The color of sunshine spots aucuba and margins the edges of sansevieria. Hinoki cypress, retinispora, and arborvitae glow with gold. Avoid using such shrubs as azalea, rhododendron, and andromeda if they have a yellow tinge for then they have a deficiency requiring that iron chelate be mixed into the soil.

Although blue is rare, spruce and Atlas cedar distinctly show this hue. Azaleas and some varieties of junipers and mahonia turn red or purple in cold weather. *Magnolia grandiflora* and leatherleaf viburnum combine green with tan or brown.

THREE SOURCES IN ONE. *Azalea branches with smooth red winter leaves complement feathery green podocarpus and rosettes of variegated* Dracaena sanderiana *in an arrangement of outdoor, florist, and indoor materials in a pillar vase.* [GARDINA]

Some indoor foliage is even more colorful, as that of rex begonias, the "painted plants." One leaf may be a rainbow of purple, silver, black, emerald, red, and rose. Begonia names like 'Merry Christmas', 'Silver Queen', 'Fireflush', 'Black Falcon', 'Green Gold', and 'Peacock' indicate the colors. The easily grown beefsteak begonia is a study in complementary red and green.

The underside of the green leaves of Moses-in-the-cradle, *Rhoeo discolor* of the spiderwort family, is a luminous purple. The spectacular markings of a bromeliad may offer an eye-catching focus for an arrangement. *Neoregelia carolinae tricolor* combines stripes of green and white with a red center. The fancy-leaved caladiums have the same striking hues. For a rich green accent, monstera and cutleaf philodendron enhance a bold design.

Visit a florist and your list grows longer. Here are green-and-red ti leaves flown from Hawaii, crimson or yellow grevillea imported from France, crotons drenched in hot colors, yellow-speckled dracaena, and silver-gray eucalyptus. Occasionally green-and-yellow flax and 'Silver King' artemisia can be found.

Textural contrasts of foliage are appropriate at holiday time. Popular then are combinations of rough needled pine and cedar, glossy holly and magnolia. Boxwood is both coarse and smooth in the bushy growth of its polished leaves. Ferns are lacy, some begonias hairy, *Anthurium clarinervum* looks like velvet. Florists carry podocarpus and pittosporum as staples because of their interesting textures as well as tropical palm and polished galax leaves.

How to Combine Foliages for green arrangements should be of similar size, but different in form and texture, mixing hues or light and dark shades. Such interaction creates the design. Thus large magnolia leaves combine poorly with ivy because of unequal size and the same color and smooth texture. Either one goes well with yew because yew is dull, dark, and shaggy. Podocarpus accented with croton creates a unique effect; begonia leaves contrast in form with yucca.

LINE AND FOCUS. *Sansevieria rosettes provide rounded form for yucca leaves, some knotted to vary shape and create a stylized design. Upturned salad bowl masquerades as base for a modern oriental compote.* [GARDINA]

Since many leaves are of linear or cluster form, a simple effective design can be made with only two kinds. The sword leaves of sansevieria set off the bird's-nest variety of the same plant. A grouping of aucuba leaves can provide focus for spears of yucca; a whorl of magnolia placed at the base of upright juniper creates a center of interest. In rare instances, one kind of leaf form suffices. The Japanese are adept at manipulating aspidistra alone into a classical design. They do this by varying heights and turning and bending the leaves to face in different directions. Ti leaves also lend themselves to such a composition.

The structure of a foliage arrangement follows the natural structure of trees and shrubs. The lines that build form follow the pattern of limbs. Shape and outline depend on their length and direction. At the perimeter, twigs are sparse and open; toward the center, growth is more compact. Look at a tree and observe how balance originates from the main line of the trunk that forms the central axis. Branches converge here creating a path that leads the eye to the heart or center of the tree.

Simple foliage designs can be made by following patterns of natural growth. Bold leaves of yucca or aspidistra or upright sprays of juniper or pine can become the central axis fixing the balance. Shorter pieces placed in secondary positions at the sides make a fuller composition that resembles more complex growth. A rounded form is usually needed in the lower area to direct the eye to the center of interest and provide a terminal point for radiating lines.

Foliage compositions look more graceful if they are not too compact. Plants need light and air to grow, so incorporate these in your artistic designs. Spaces help to separate forms and emphasize shapes.

Color variations can be used to create highlights and shadows. By recessing dark leaves and bringing lighter ones to the fore a series of planes is created that pulls the eye back into the design and thus suggests depth. As a rule, darker or brighter leaves are placed toward the base of a design to stabilize it. Light-colored leaves in the upper areas help prevent top-heaviness. Gradations from pale to dark move the eye through the design toward the center of interest.

Grooming   The Groooming of leaves is always important but especially so in all-green designs where soiled leaves or spray residue are blemishes quickly noticed. Oiling or waxing foliage does not help since it destroys the natural sheen that is preferable to a commercial polish. To cleanse foliage, in a mild soap bath, swish it then rub off dirt with paper toweling. Rinse well in clear cool water and dry, then polish leaves to a rich gloss with a soft cloth.

When my own garden is sprayed professionally, I forbid the use of oil-base insecticides since these mar leaves irreparably. Instead, water mixtures are used. Since these are easily washed off by rain, spraying must be done on a dry day when there is no threat of precipitation.

When you want an entire house plant for an arrangement, remove the pot and wash all the soil from the roots, taking care not to break them. A cluster-type plant like *Rhoeo discolor* or a bromeliad (or individual leaves of aspidistra or stalks of angel-wing begonia separated from the parent) can then be easily stationed on a holder or, if necessary, first attached to a balsa wood stick for support. When the arrangement is dismantled, the plant can be repotted or sometimes, as with sansevieria, pieces rooted in water.

12

ARRANGEMENTS THAT LAST

Fall heralds the season for dried arrangements. Weeds, vegetables, fruits, flowers, and foliages collected from the roadside, market, and garden offer an abundance of material. Treated with special agents, the beauty of many plants can be preserved almost indefinitely. Offering a wide variety of shapes and textures, dried flowers and foliages often retain their bright colors and those that do fade can be revitalized with spray paint or gilding.

Success with dried arrangements involves three things: selection of suitable material, application of the proper processing method—hanging, burying, or absorption—and the use of adequate mechanics.

Natural Drying   Many plants dry naturally as part of their life cycle. The tall, brown stalks of mullein, thistle, teasel, heracleum (cow-parsnip), sumac (not the poisonous kind), dock, and cattails may be picked when dry and used without treatment, except perhaps for an application of plastic spray to prevent heracleum from shattering, and dipping cattails in undiluted shellac to forestall their blasting. Most of these wild plants make excellent line materials for structuring an arrangement.

You can also find interesting pods on the ground beneath black locust, empress or paulownia trees, the sycamore, and, of course, many kinds of cones from needled evergreens.

Astilbes, seed clusters of ornamental onion or leek (*Allium*), and yarrow from the garden also dry naturally, but take care to harvest these before they deteriorate. Then color browns and seed-heads shrink and disintegrate. It is better to pick prematurely than to delay, for drying can be completed in the house by hanging or by propping stems in a deep, empty tin can.

By Hanging   Plants to dry indoors by hanging include acacia, artemisia, banana, bird-of-paradise and rubber-plant leaves, bells-of-Ireland, cacti (stand upright), ochra stalks, ornamental grasses, palm, pepper berries, protea, snowball hydrangea, statice, strawflowers, and sunflowers (petals removed). Globe thistle (*Echinops*), liatris, and Queen-Anne's-lace can be dried by hanging but retain better color if buried in an agent. Lotus leaves dry naturally on the plant but I prefer them glycerinized (see Chapter 5). When hanging flowers, remove foliage, tie in bunches, and suspend heads down from a clothesline, coat hanger, or drying rack in a cool, airy darkened place. I use my basement. Unlike flowers for fresh arrangements, which are cut early morning or late afternoon, materials for drying are gathered during sunny hours, and never when wet with rain or dew. Darkness is necessary during the drying process, since flowers fade in bright light.

With crested celosia, place the heads upside down in a paper bag and tie it shut. This way you catch the seed for next year's bloom and also preserve color. So treated, red and pink celosia hold their colors but the yellows and greens of the gold types fade and it seems impossible to retain these hues. Approximately three weeks of drying time is needed.

Blue hydrangeas are useful for bulk as well as focal areas in designs. Although they can be air-dried, they have more vibrancy if stood in a receptacle with an inch and a half of water and let dry as the water evaporates. This method also works well with plumed celosia and such exotics as bird-of-paradise flowers, protea, and ginger.

To Dry Artichokes and Fruits

Choice items to dry can also be found among fruits and vegetables. Artichokes have long been favorites; they can be gilded, shellacked, or painted for use in seasonal holiday decorations. Artichokes can be processed either closed or in rosette form. Left alone in a safe place, the closed artichoke dries naturally. Do not refrigerate at all.

To obtain the rosette form, plunge the artichoke briefly into boiling water. Spread the leaves apart until the small thistles of the heart are visible. Press the artichoke face-down on a hard surface covered with paper toweling to absorb moisture. Taking care to have leaves flat and straight, replace with dry towels as needed. During the two to three weeks of drying, flatten the artichoke periodically with the heel of your hand so as to hold the rosette form.

In winter, this procedure works well if the flattened artichoke is placed under the cover of a hot radiator. To vary the rosette form, stuff strips of paper toweling between the leaves, drop melted paraffin into the base of each layer to prevent complete closing, or prop leaves open with toothpicks. For a closed rosette, you can also bend leaves inward, tucking the tips between the layers. To station on a needle-holder, insert a stake in the stem end of the artichoke before it dries.

Lemons, limes, nuts, pomegranates, small hot red peppers, even whole pineapples (not just the leaves) can also be dried. It is important that the fruit be firm, unblemished, and not too ripe. A large, airy closet with the door ajar or a darkened corner makes an ideal area for spreading the fruit on a cake rack and letting nature take its course. For pineapples, slide a pan under the rack to catch any seeping juices. The fruit should not be discarded if it becomes soft for it will harden again. Six weeks or more are required to turn the fruit to a mellow beige shade. Pomegranates dry a dull reddish-

DRIED FRUITS AND VEGETABLES. *Roadside fasciated mullein and glycerinized aspidistra leaves provide height for a large fungus as background mass. This sets off a grouping of air-dried corn-husk rosettes, nuts, limes, pomegranates, pineapples, and artichokes.* [SUTER]

DRAMATIC YET HARMONIOUS. *In a perfect blending of textures, forms, and shades of tan, a fasciated stem of celosia, two glycerinized lotus leaves, and lichen catch and hold attention.* [SUTER]

brown, and are more effective if sprayed red and antiqued with gold. Limes and lemons can be treated the same way.

To anchor these fruits in an arrangement, stick a thumbtack in the stem end before the drying process is completed. Then fasten a 6-inch length of 22-gauge wire under the head of each tack, gluing it in place. With the wire, you can attach the fruit to stakes for stationing in an arrangement, or you can wire fruit before it dries according to directions in Chapter 14.

Recently, I experimented with cherry or kidney beans and discovered after wiring and displaying them fresh in an arrangement, they dried well, turning a soft tan. Red hot Italian peppers should also be wired in bunches before drying. (See Chapter 14 and follow as directions for string beans.)

To Dry Flowers   For fragile garden flowers, dry by burying in a special agent as silica gel or, my favorite, a mixture of equal parts of borax and yellow cornmeal. Directions for silica gel, sold under one trade name as Flower-Dri, are given on the can, but the procedure for borax and cornmeal is slightly different. Here is the method I use:

1. Pick flowers in the afternoon on a dry day, never when wet with rain or dew, or after standing in water in an arrangement. Process immediately. Select only those in prime condition or just before maturity.

2. Cut off stems to within an inch of flower heads.

3. Strip off any remaining foliage.

4. To make a false stem, dip the end of a length of 22-gauge wire in Elmer's glue, insert into the base of flower head close to the stem, and tape the two together.

5. Line a shoe or dress box with wax paper.

6. Prepare drying mixture of equal parts of borax and yellow cornmeal. Add 3 tablespoons uniodized salt per quart of mixture for better color preservation.

En Masse. *For mass design, a greater amount of dried material than fresh is needed to fill the same space.* [SUTER]

7. Cover the bottom of the lined box with a half-inch layer of the mixture.

8. Place each flower face-up in the box. Bend wire far enough below head so blossom lies flat. Straighten wire when ready to use the flowers. Mound-up mixture underneath head to cushion it.

9. Gently sift mixture between petals, adding until sides and top are just covered but not buried deeply. Never dry more than a single layer of flowers in a box and leave room for mixture between heads. Do not crowd.

10. Leave box open without lid. Check process after 5 to 7 days. Do not leave in mixture when dry.

11. To dry spikey flowers such as liatris, lay lengthwise and use natural stem.

12. When flowers are dry, brush away mixture, and to remove, slide your hand gently under each head, lifting it on your outstretched fingers. Lay the flower *on top* of the mixture and let rest

LIGHT AS A FEATHER. *A quantity of dried material will fit in a container with a relatively small opening because stems are thin and heads are light.* [SUTER]

for at least 24 hours to firm up petals. This step is extremely important, for unless blossoms are allowed this undisturbed respite in the air, petals will shatter. Once cured, they can be sprayed lightly with a plastic coating for security.

13. Keep processed flowers in closed boxes on tissue paper until needed.

14. Store mixture in tightly covered tins to reuse the following seasons.

SUITABLE FLOWERS FOR BURYING:

aster	gladiolus	marigold	snapdragon
daffodil	liatris	peony	stock
dahlia	lilac	Queen-Anne's-lace	tulip
delphinium	lily	rose	zinnia
Echinops			

(*Note:* Roses, if full-blown, fall apart, so pick for drying when about two-thirds open.)

For Foliage   Many foliages can be preserved with glycerine. Leaves are transformed to a rich brown, but remain soft and pliable. Water is no longer needed to maintain freshness, and if foliage has been in water before glycerinizing, the process may not be successful. Foliages that respond well include garden, florist, and house plant materials and these are especially recommended:

aucuba	copper beech
aspidistra (also can be air-dried)	elaeagnus
boxwood	euonymus (*E. alatus* and *japonica*)
cocculus (Snailseed—one of	ivy
the florist's prettiest)	laurel

leatherleaf viburnum	papyrus
leucothoe	peony
magnolia (*M. grandiflora*	plum
and *virginiana*)	sorrel tree
mahonia	winterhazel

Treat only freshly cut branches, and avoid soft, new growth. Split or crush the stems for several inches to speed absorption. Prepare a mixture of 1 part glycerine (from a drug store) to 2 parts warm water. (Some people recommend undiluted anti-freeze, but it turns foliage black.) Pour mixture to a depth of 4 to 5 inches in a 1-pound coffee can or plastic bucket. Stand branches up in this but completely submerge ivy. Store in a dark, cool place for about 3 weeks. When beads of glycerine begin to appear on the leaves, absorption is completed. Remove branches and hang upside-down to allow solution *within* the stem to work down to the tip. This sometimes rescues top foliage that has withered before absorption has taken place. Do not leave branches in solution longer than necessary. To prevent mold from forming, add a few drops of Clorox to the mixture. The solution is reusable.

Bleaching and Dyeing

I have often admired dried materials bleached commercially in Japan. Mrs. Toku Sugiyama, who has watched and practiced this process, has kindly shared her knowledge with me. She uses a solution of 1 cup Clorox to 2½ to 3 gallons of water but cautions to add more water if you can smell the Clorox. Too strong a solution causes material to disintegrate. Always wear gloves. Material to be bleached must first be air-dried by hanging. Mrs. Sugiyama begins with fresh foliage, cleanses it in clear water, and then hangs it in the sun out-of-doors for about 10 days. If it rains, she brings it inside. When materials are completely dry, she places foliage in Clorox solution, using a plastic bucket, glass vessel, or crock, but not an aluminum or other metal container. Weight foliage down with another bucket on top filled with water. Soak at least 10 days, but check periodically and remove promptly when bleaching has occurred. Foliage must then be *thoroughly* rinsed and washed with clear water, and left in a clear bath for a day or two. Hang it up again outside to let the sun dry and whiten it.

To dye bleached foliage, do not hang to dry after the clear bath, but dip for about 5 minutes in a boiling Ritz solution, mixed according to the directions on the package. Wash thoroughly after dyeing, then dry, but not in the sun.

Materials suitable for bleaching include many of those air-dried. Aspidistra and bird-of-paradise leaves are suggested foliages, grape and wisteria vines bleach well but must first be peeled; for flowers, try bells-of-Ireland and sunflowers, also roadside thistle. Materials with seed-heads are not recommended nor any fragile leaves.

Mechanics   Use Oasis, sand, or chicken wire in the container when you are constructing a dried arrangement. I like Oasis best, but slightly dampened sand can be substituted and hardens as it dries. Or you can pour a layer of paraffin on top of the sand when arrangement is completed. Some arrangers recommend Styrofoam, but holes must be punched first with an ice pick for thin or fragile stems. This is not necessary if heavier 18-gauge wire is used for false stems. For heavy flowers and foliage, chicken wire will be needed. (See Chapter 4 for directions in measuring and fitting to a container.)

Many dried materials are available commercially and the list grows longer each year. But when you plant your garden, consider including some flowers and foliages of your own to dry for your autumn arrangements.

To make contrived flowers and learn other methods of drying, here are books you may find helpful. *The Art of Drying Plants and*

Flowers by Mabel Squires (M. Barrows & Co., Inc., New York, 1958—out of print); *Creative Designs with Dried and Contrived Flowers* by Esther Veramae Hamél (Simon and Schuster, New York, 1971); and *Forever Flowers* by Rejean Metzler (Charles Scribner's Sons, 1972).

13

WAYS WITH WEATHERED WOOD

In flower arrangement, driftwood is viewed as natural sculpture. Its dramatic form, pleasing color, and interesting texture complement many plant materials to create distinctive designs. Driftwood, commonly used to refer to tree forms found along the shore, is really part of a much larger category known as weathered wood. Included are such related forms as roots, fungi, branches, and stumps that can be found inland as well as near water.

Most woods reflect their habitat and their characteristics are often as different as their origins. The sleek, volumetric configuration of a cypress knee toned to a rich mahogany is as unlike the buff-colored pierced structure of cholla wood as are their homes, Florida and New Mexico. Manzanita and juniper share only the affiliation of being trees.

Where to Find   Although weathered wood does not qualify as living material, the dried forms suggest its former vitality. Carved by wind, water, and rock, it has been aged by the seasons and by the sun. Sought for display, fun, or profit, specimens can be found along beaches, river banks, lake shores, inlets, and coves; on construction sites, in the desert or woods, possibly in your own backyard. Weathered wood may also be bought in shops specializing in floral equipment and unusual gifts.

The hunting season for this natural sculpture peaks in summer. With saw, pruning shears, and a discerning eye, the collector prepares for the recovery of small and large quarry. When a coveted piece is too cumbersome to carry, desirable portions are salvaged by on-the-spot removal. If the search is timed for the aftermath of a storm, prospects are greater.

How to Treat   Driftwood may emerge as a completed work of art. Clean and shining, it needs no refinement. However, shape may be altered by removing some portions and relocating them to improve height or balance, by adding segments to increase size, or by combining two or more pieces to produce a more complex form. Although the finish seldom needs retouching, surface highlights may be developed by shading with one or more tones of pastel chalk, and this is easily washed off if the effect doesn't suit. For permanence, a coat of clear plastic spray is recommended. A unique effect is possible if melted candle wax in mixed colors is dribbled over selected areas. A light application of water-soluble paint may be attractive but enamel, varnish, or wax obscures the natural luster.

Wood forms found inland usually need considerable grooming. Partially decayed and covered with dirt, they require strong hosing, scraping with a stiff wire brush and chisel, or soaking and scrubbing with soap and water. Sometimes the cleaning must be repeated several times. Sanding the surface improves texture; varnish, stain, or wax accentuates grain and color. Shoe polish makes an effective finish, and black or white lacquer produces dramatic contrasts for modern settings.

As sculptural characteristics become visible, the form is studied from all sides to determine possible reshaping and mounting. If sections must be removed and relocated, epoxy glue serves as a bonding agent. Metal rods or sections of wire coat hangers can also join segments. Inserted into holes drilled into the wood, and prop-

FROM THE BACK YARD. *Almost alone, roots and dead branches make a complete design requiring only two rhododendron blossoms for color and freshness.* [SUTER]

A New Relationship. *Here a form of weathered wood resembles an iron crane, and leatherleaf viburnum follows and accents the lower contour.* [SUTER]

erly fitted, they adhere without gluing, making it easy to disassemble a large piece.

Natural sculpture may need leveling with a wedge or with children's blocks. As filler for uneven areas, these may be permanently attached to the underside with glue, screws, or nails.

Sometimes the bottom must be cut to make it level. A water mark can establish the line for a straight edge. Held at the desired angle, a piece is dipped into a pail of water to the depth of the unwanted section. The saw then follows the line that divides wet from dry.

Bases and Mechanics

Natural sculpture usually looks best set on a base. Lumberyards are a convenient source for unfinished boards; they will cut them to specification. Suitable materials include: particle board, a composition of chips and shavings known as Novaply; Versa or Flake board; No. 2 white pine shelving, available in one-by-ten, or one-

(ABOVE) VALENTINES FOR A LUNCHEON IN RED AND WHITE. *The colors of the felt cloth topped with lace doilies and runner, the milk glass compote containers, Italian pottery plates studded with fake jewels, ruby Fostoria goblets are all repeated in the twin fresh floral bouquets. The size of the table determines the proportion and scale of the arrangement.* [KLENDER] *See page* 182. (BELOW) FALL MEANS THANKSGIVING. *Balance is crucial in Buffet tables, in this instance achieved by appointments of comparable size, visual weight, and character. Brass and copper make an harmonious mix on a linen cloth whose color repeats their finishes. Plum foliage and fresh garden flowers in fall colors suggest the pattern of the Lenox china.* [KLENDER] *See page* 186. (TOP RIGHT) TRADITIONAL YET CURRENT. *Container and arrangement unify yet contrast with place settings. Belgium linen and lace place mats carry out the spirit of Wedgwood china and candlesticks, all Semiformal in character. Blue is the dominant color.* [KLENDER] *See page* 183. (BOTTOM RIGHT) IT'S SPRING. *A minimum of appointments in a Semiformal Functional setting relieves the table of clutter. Though mats are plastic and plates are earthenware, they nevertheless have an understated elegance compatible with the antique Meissen vases. The setting is fresh and crisp, but with feminine appeal. Flatware would be omitted in a flower show and candles would not be appropriate for a luncheon setting.* [KLENDER]. *See page* 184.

THE GLITTER OF NEW YEAR'S. *New, tasteful, and modish, this Exhibition Segment has everything going for it as a winner. Glass and plastic combine to make a foil for a gold lamé backdrop, muting it and at the same time reflecting its brilliance.* [KLENDER] *See page 189.*

SCULPTURE IN MIXED MEDIA. *Relaxing rules, a free-style composition incorporates driftwood, glass slag, feather rock, and anthurium in a sculpture that appeals to the Sogetsu Master.* [KLENDER] *See page 202.*

OHARA INFLUENCE. *Dried orange palm frames fresh yellow daylilies and ligularia leaves in a bold moribana design.* [SUTER] *See page 202.*

CASUAL GRACE. *This is a typical conventional design— harmonious, decorative, and without conflict.* [SUTER] *See page 205.*

UNMISTAKABLY FRENCH. *In an eighteenth-century setting with typical rococo colors, this arrangement does not interfere with the painting above and fits the shape of the antique vase of slightly later date by Jacob Petit. Painting, "Marquise De Besons," by Jean-Baptiste Greuze, 1725–1805, Baltimore Museum of Art.* [SUTER] *See page 213.*

HOMEY AND CAREFREE. *An unstudied mixed bouquet in an old bean pot brightens an early American setting. Eltonhead Manor Room, circa 1750, Baltimore Museum of Art.* [SUTER] *See page 215.*

STABILE. *In frozen movement, wooden hoops and weathered wood have characteristics of actual motion. Without motorizing them, inert lines appear to weave in and out of space.* [KLENDER] *See page 234.*

FLUORESCENCE. *A lamp base, weathered wood, allium and palm sprayed with fluorescent paint take on new character under black light.* [SUTER] *See page 238.*

MULTICOLORED LIGHT. *My objective of overlapping a combination of colored lights on a white arrangement of fresh material was accomplished by following Faber Birren's instructions. Three 150-watt stained-glass spots (150 PAR 38/SP/6G green, 150 PAR 38/SP/6B blue, 150 PAR 38/SP/6R red) in swivel sockets were spaced 7 to 8 inches apart, center on center. Shining them on the white arrangement against a white background produced brilliant shadows in red, yellow, and turquoise. [SUTER] See page 239.*

STAINED GLASS. *Light and stained glass are natural companions. An amber spotlight directed from behind the sculpture increases its vitality. Sculpture by Frieda Friedman. [SUTER] See page 239.*

SHIMMER OF SILVER. *Mirrors add sparkle to the luster of plasticized paper molded in free form. Under light, begonia leaves gleam; even gerberas seem to shine* [ARAUJO] *See page 239.*

HARMONY VERSUS CACOPHONY. *Illustrating how color can unify patterns and shapes of opposing character, this design brought the author the 1971 "Flower Arranger of the Year," Helen S. Hull trophy, awarded by the National Council of State Garden Clubs.* [KLENDER] *See page 244.*

URBAN RENEWAL. *Discarded building materials add dimension to a modern architectural sculpture accented with dried artichokes and a banana leaf, related in color and texture, all integrated in a design "on target" for the theme.* [KLENDER] *See page 247.*

VIGNETTE. *The furnishings and color scheme of an entire room are represented in this small section which appeared on the author's television series, "The Flower Show." Courtesy, Maryland Center for Public Broadcasting.* [YUSAITIS] *See page 258.*

ALWAYS A WINNER. *The single dahlia 'Jem' (originated in 1972 by Mrs. J. Edgar Miller), here perfectly associated with the spectacular sorrel-tree, wins a tricolor whenever it is exhibited* [KLENDER] *See page 274.*

STILL-LIFE. *Here are forms and colors worthy of a painter—echinops, gloriosa daisies, and tritoma in a copper pitcher.* [SUTER] *See page 274.*

by-twelve sizes. Boards may be varnished or stained to suit the sculpture. Paint, shoe polish, adhesive-backed paper, or a covering of rough-textured fabric like burlap or felt offer other methods of finishing. Straw mats, cork, and such natural materials as burls, cork, teak, bamboo, and slate in geometric or irregular shapes are other possibilities. For an oriental effect, a piece of weathered wood might be set on a bed of Japanese stone held in place by a rope border.

If the wood suggests a figure, it may look well elevated on a wooden dowel or metal rod, which has been sunk into a wooden block of sufficient dimensions and weight to support it. Fir lumber measuring four-by-four, or six-by-six square can be cut to any length for this purpose.

Commercial devices are also available for anchoring driftwood

LIKE EACH OTHER. *In texture and color, driftwood and dried wisteria are so like the Aztec container that they seem to be an extension of it. Winterhazel foliage has similar qualities, but peonies introduce a different note.* [SUTER]

MECHANICS REVEALED. *A flat metal disc screwed into the base of driftwood provides a stable seat. Heavy branches may be wrapped at the base with hardware-cloth tied on with wire, or screwed to an inverted needle-holder (made for this purpose), and then impaled on another holder, teeth interlocking.* [SUTER]

LAND AND SEA. *In combination with marine forms of sea fans, coral, and sponges, a root and twisted grape vine make a simple but forceful composition.* [MALASHUK]

IT'S A NATURAL. *Iris flowers and foliage, giant alliums and hosta leaves are at home in a log container.* [SUTER]

in a container or on a base. Made of heavy metal, one type resembles a flat disc, while the other has needle points attached to the underside, which lock into a conventional needle-holder. Both mechanics fasten to the wood with accompanying screws. Melted paraffin also stations wood in containers. To station a branch, wrap the end two or three times with a strip of hardware cloth about two to three inches wide (size depending on length and weight of branch), and fasten it with 22-gauge wire laced through the holes. Let the hardware cloth extend below the end of the branch so as to insert it in the needle-holder.

Floral designs incorporating weathered wood make interesting decorations for the home. The wood may be used as container, accessory, or a sculptural focus depending on size and shape. As most pieces are of strong form, they combine well with bold plant materials. Weathered wood is versatile combining well with most fresh flowers and such dried materials as sunflowers, hydrangeas, celosia, and banksia. Hosta, palm, caladium, aspidistra, and yucca leaves; also leaf and needled evergreens are good companions. Fruits and vegetables, coral and water plants, industrial and technological products, as metals and plastics, are also suitable.

Wood forms with pockets or openings can function as containers. However since they will not hold water for fresh material, a cupholder, a tin can, or glass jar with a needle-holder is wedged inside with floral clay. Pre-soaked Oasis is inserted in irregular openings; tubes or florist picks, wired to the wood or fastened with floral clay, are used in small openings for only one or two flowers.

Designs featuring wood scultpure may have flowers at the base, the rear or side, or on the surface, these supported in a cupholder or a container placed in an auxiliary position. To affix flowers to a wood surface, wrap wet Oasis with chicken wire and fasten it at the seam with florist wire. Then you can tie the mechanic in any position to the wood placing blooms at different angles and thus diversifying the design.

14

FRUITS AND VEGETABLES FOR
A CHANGE

Arrangements featuring fresh fruits and vegetables tease the eye and tempt the palate. They also appeal to the pocketbook because they can be served as food after they have served as decoration. Colorful and succulent, fruits and vegetables offer a wide variety of forms and textures for distinctive designs. Each season suggests a characteristic mood—bare branches and evergreen boughs for winter, budding foliage for spring, masses of bright flowers juxtaposed with water for hot-weather summer designs, and for autumn the abundance of the harvest.

When you plan to use fruits and vegetables, consider the variety of available forms. I keep a list for reference, adding to it when I visit the market as the seasons change. This helps me to plan arrangements as I picture forms, colors, shapes, and textures.

Take squash for example. There are enough varieties of shapes and colors to make a fine arrangement with this vegetable alone. Butternut, yellow squash, and zucchini are forms with the same elongated bodies but with different colors—tan, yellow, and green. In the acorn family one elliptical form has a dark green fluted surface accented with orange; the white squash is a flat scalloped disc. Necks of squashes are crooked or straight, their skin textures rough

MAINSTAYS. *Pineapple and cabbage are basic to fruit and vegetable arrangement contributing height, bulk, and focus.* [SUTER]

or smooth, their hues pale, dark, bright or streaked. A sampling can make a dramatic design.

Choose fruits and vegetables that are fresh and free of blemish. Avoid perishable ones, such as lettuce and strawberries that are likely to wilt or rot without refrigeration. Slightly green produce lasts longer than when it is overly ripe. Test for firmness, but don't bruise. Avoid cut fruits and vegetables, even though they do add interest, for they deteriorate rapidly and attract insects.

Values in Forms   When planning an arrangement, you will find it helpful to divide fruits and vegetables into characteristic groups. Such mainstays as cabbage, eggplant, pineapple, small pumpkin, and large squashes have good form, color, and lasting qualities. They are basic to many designs because of their size and interesting shapes; they provide a foundation for fastening other materials with floral picks and also establish height and focus.

Then there is the round medium-sized group of fruits and vegetables useful for filling out and developing a design. Having the same visual and good keeping qualities are apples, artichokes, avocado, beets, bell peppers, coconut, kohlrabi, mangos, papaya, pears, persimmons, pomegranates, squash, turnips, and yellow and red Italian onions.

For height, there are such elongated types as carrots, corn,

Who's This? *An Indian mask carries out a fruit and vegetable theme yet provides new interest.* [GARDINA]

cucumbers, finger-shaped sweet peppers, horseradish root, parsnips, red or green bananas, salsify (oyster plant), yellow squash, and zucchini. These may also be worked into the body of the design.

Best used in clusters are the smaller fruits and vegetables including Brussels sprouts, cranberries, diminutive eggplants, cherry or kidney beans, garlic, grapes, kumquats, lady apples, limes, mushrooms, new potatoes, nuts, okra, red or white radishes, Seckel pears, small red or green hot peppers, and string beans. Strung on wire and then bunched, these smaller forms can cascade over the lip of a container to soften its edge, rest on a base as transition to the design, or they can fill in spaces left by uneven shapes placed side by side, or piled in a mound, or they can crown the top like the star on a Christmas tree.

Some fruits and vegetables are rather difficult to use. Oranges, lemons, yellow bananas, and grapefruit are difficult to integrate because of their bold colors, but grapefruit does provide a mechanic. It can be concealed and forms impaled upon it. Most melons are too bulky and plums, peaches, strawberries, cherries and tomatoes, except when green, almost impossible to wire and they ripen quickly and are likely to mash. Leafy materials—collard, lettuce, rhubarb, chard, and spinach—wilt at room temperature; but some may stay fresh if hardened first by submerging. Asparagus, broccoli, cauliflower, celery, lima beans, and peas please some arrangers but seem to me to lack visual appeal, although purple broccoli is, indeed, an oddity.

Color is important in fruit and vegetable designs; hues should be varied but compatible. Purples, blues, and reds combine well because they are related. Shades of green are harmonious, and yellow, tan, orange, and brown rarely clash. Dark colors accent pale or brighter tones, but a monotonous design results with all the same shades. If eggplant, purple cabbage, and blue grapes are used, the addition of turnips, red radishes, and pomegranates creates a brighter composition than darker-toned beets, cranberries, and red onions. An all-tan scheme of parsnips, salsify, butternut squash, and russet pears is bland but it can be pepped up with a pumpkin, a pineapple, and kumqauts.

Since many fruits and vegetables have a glossy surface they shine naturally if washed, wiped clean, and buffed with a soft cloth as you blow on them. (Artificial polishes destroy natural "bloom" and material so treated is usually penalized in a flower show.) Take care not to stand them in water, which hastens deterioration.

Containers and Mechanics

Various containers suit fruits and vegetables. Footed compotes make attractive centerpieces; compositions may be built on reed mats, wooden slabs, plaques, and bases. Epergnes are traditional favorites for their elegance, crocks and basins for their simplicity. Trays, casseroles, celery and vegetable dishes may be pressed into service. Baskets, cornucopias, and scales have long been popular, also ornamental boxes with the lids raised.

For work with fruits and vegetables, you may need, in addition to your clippers, needle-holders and clay, stakes, chicken wire (or wire netting), sections of wire clothes hangers, florist picks, and wire (18- and 22-gauge), also Twist-Ems, wire cutters, an ice pick, hammer, water tubes, and pliers. The needle-holder and clay will firmly support arrangements. Florist picks and wire ties prevent rolling. Stakes can make false stems or reinforce natural ones. A cushion of crushed chicken wire or brown paper underneath forms elevates them in a deep container and florist picks or wire clothes hanger sections serve to impale a pear, for example, on a pumpkin. An ice pick is invaluable for piercing fruits and vegetables so you can insert wires for stringing and bunching. With pliers you can twist wires tight to lock forms in place.

Stakes and Wiring

For stakes, cut fresh, sturdy branches of rose-of-Sharon, privet, or comparable shrub. Don't use dead wood as it is brittle and breaks under the weight of an arrangement. Cut sections about one-quarter

TECHNIQUES WITH FRUITS AND VEGETABLES. *1. Apple with hook at base to catch into bud end. 2. Grapes cradled in "V" forked stake. 3. Apples wired to a green rose-of-Sharon stake. 4. Grapes with a Twist-Em through center of stem. 5. "V" fork stake. 6. First step in wiring lime: Insert wire horizontally below stem end. 7. Second step: Bend up short and long end of wire and twist locking lime in place. 8. First step in bunching radishes: Attach one radish to each end of 22-gauge wire as for limes, bend wire near center so radishes hang at uneven lengths. 9. Radishes wired into a bunch ready for attaching to a stake on holder as in number three.* [KLENDER]

inch thick and long enough to equal the height of the proposed composition. You can always cut stakes back if they show when the piece is finished. Remove interfering side shoots but save a branch with a "V" at the top for this can support a quantity of material in various positions. A forked stake can also make a frame from which to hang bunches of grapes or to cradle them.

To wire an apple, pierce it with an ice pick vertically through the core from the stem hollow through the blossom end. Insert a strand of 18-gauge wire, 9 to 12 inches long, so that half an inch protrudes from the base of the apple and the rest of the wire extends from the top. Bend the short end into a hook and carefully draw it back until it just catches into the base of the apple. The apple now hangs and the long end of wire can be wrapped to a stake already in place on a needle-holder. If a close-in placement is desired, the apple can be wired tightly against the stake, or you can drop the apple over the edge of a container by slackening the wire. Two or three apples can be tied at different levels.

To wire lemons or limes, run an ice pick *horizontally* through the end, but far enough below the tip to prevent the wire from tearing the skin open and breaking free when the wire is twisted to lock the fruit in place. As with the apple, you should have a short and a long end of wire, but instead of making a hook with the short end, you will bend both ends up and twist the short piece to the longer one looping the fruit in place. It then hangs and is attached to a stake as before.

Nuts, radishes, and Brussels sprouts are wired as are limes but with 22-gauge wire, one vegetable hanging at each end. The wire is bent near the center like a hairpin, but in uneven lengths, and

CLUSTERS FOR GRACE. *Sprigs of ligustrum soften a mound of purple cabbage, turnips, eggplant, and a pomegranate. Radishes and kidney beans wired in bunches add a finishing touch.* [SUTER]

FROM MY GARDEN. *Leaves of horseradish, ornamental cabbage, and onions look prettier than they taste.* [SUTER]

several wires are twisted together to make a cluster, and this is attached to a stake. An ice pick will not penetrate hard-shelled butternuts and walnuts; these must be drilled.

String beans can be strung on 22-gauge wire like beads, the ends of the wire twisted together and two or more bunches joined. When wiring fruits and vegetables, turn stem ends in toward the interior of a design, and the blossom ends facing the viewer.

Tie large forms like pineapples or eggplants to a stake by wrapping a Twist-Em or fine wire around the necks under leaves or stems. Fasten the bottom to a base with clay. With fruits and vegetables, avoid using wire that is so heavy it causes tears.

To station linear cucumbers, parsnips, or zucchini in upright positions for a tall design, force them onto stakes or florist picks and insert these on a needle-holder.

Select bunches of grapes that hang loosely. Catch through the center with a Twist-Em to distribute their weight and so avoid breaks. Or support a bunch on a forked branch. This is particularly useful as you can hang or wire materials on both sides of an arrangement, and, of course, "Y" stake holds more.

To compose a fruit and vegetable arrangement on a base or board, first fasten a needle-holder near the back with clay. Be sure holder and clay are dry. Hammer a stake already cut to the correct length onto the center of the holder and test for stability. If the stake comes out easily when you pull on it, your design will be doomed. Sometimes one strong stake suffices to support an entire composition, especially when a "Y" stake is used.

Place a large form like a pineapple or eggplant in a slightly slanted position so it leans against the stake. Tie it in place at the neck and secure the bottom to the base with a wad of clay. Add another large form, a cabbage or a second pineapple, in a horizontal position. For a tall design, insert linear material, as foliage sprays or tall leaves at the back. Build up the arrangement with medium-sized fruits and vegetables. Let bunches hang from the top or spill over the front, and finish off with small individual fruits or vegetables to conceal mechanics. Fill in any spaces with sprigs of ivy or other foliage which will stay fresh if it is inserted in water tubes. The greens act as transition between forms.

When you assemble fruits and vegetables for decoration, store them in a cool *safe* place. If your family is like mine, they may consume important materials before you have time to arrange them!

15

SETTING THE TABLE FOR COMPLIMENTS

A famous hostess once said to me, "You can tell what I think of my guests by the way I set my table. For my dearest friends I use my finest appointments. Second best is good enough for most people and nondescript plates and glasses are adequate for the family." In one of her columns, an art critic wrote that she was content with glassware prizes from the gas station and dishes from the hardware store, no matter what the occasion, company included. These attitudes fail to recognize table setting as an art.

When guests enter a dining room and see a beautifully appointed table or a whimsically imaginative one, admiration is spontaneous. An exceptional setting can make such a lasting impression that it is remembered long after the occasion when food and companions are forgotten. I recall one notable setting. The hostess had combined Mexican tinware with blue linen place mats. Blueberry soup was served in colorful bowls that looked like sea horses. The centerpiece featured comical masks also of tin, blue hydrangeas from the garden, and dried curls of wisteria painted to match. The coordination of appointments was so unusual that guests voiced approval instantly.

Once when I visited an elderly dowager and walked through her handsome dining room with its French eighteenth-century banquet table and chest inlaid with Sèvres plaques, I noticed in the sunny bay window a small table set for four for luncheon. Apricot-bordered white plates rested on yellow-flowered organdy mats. A white ceramic basket filled with fragrant freesias, yellow iris, orange-and-green parrot tulips, and a quantity of ivy made the centerpiece. For this lady, I was sure that a gracious table setting was a way of life.

An exhibition table in a flower show was striking both for simplicity and boldness. Surprisingly, all the appointments were of plastic. The exhibitor had fashioned the purple cloth from Indian Head cotton, and trimmed it with two bands of awning fabric striped in yellow, orange, green, and white. The bands crossed the width of each side of center. Four square, traylike white plates, holding round purple dishes, were placed two on each band and opposite each other. Cups, saucers, and napkins were also purple. At the

HALLOWEEN. *When you set a table, plan a design. Centerpiece and candles in off-center composition balance each other. For Halloween, an Indian mask, framed with hydrangeas to simulate hair, is accented with fresh fruits and vegetables in keeping with the season. Well-related appointments express the same casual mood.* [KLENDER]

ends of the table, a pair of L-shaped orange ceramic containers each held two fresh palmetto leaves and two coral anthuriums. The effect was dramatic, for the exhibitor had made commonplace appointments appear distinctive by beautifully correlating them.

Poorly set tables also leave memories. For a buffet supper for her husband's associates, a banker's wife covered the table with a lovely old cloth of linen cutwork. For the centerpiece without flowers she used a modern, black, wrought-iron candelabra. The platters and serving dishes were a conglomeration of silver, plastic, and wood. Surely this hostess was either inept or indifferent. In a museum-sponsored show, one young matron, recently married into a wealthy family, attracted unfortunate attention. Her appalling display included a lace cloth, a hand-chased silver tea and coffee service, silver candelabra, and an epergne of fresh fruit. On matching platters with these handsome appointments were hot dogs, a head of cauliflower, and a stack of corncobs—all cooked. From the incongruity of menu and appointments, it was not clear if the occasion was a high tea or a barbecue. To make matters worse, the food deteriorated during the day-long exhibition.

When you set a table, it's a good idea to plan a design just as you do when you arrange flowers. Admittedly, a table setting is more complex for it must harmoniously relate plant materials with certain colors, textures, and styles of appointments—china, glassware, flatware, and linens. Although neatness is a mark of excellence in all design,. it is especially important in table settings where inappropriate or carelessly placed appointments can mar a display.

For many years, table settings were classified by the quality of tableware and cloth and the ratio between number of guests and people serving them. To qualify as a Formal seated dinner, a table required elegant appointments and a symmetrical design of place settings. No bread-and-butter plates were ever included; there was wine and, of course, service plates. At least one waiter or waitress was essential for every three or four diners.

For Semiformal seated dinners, the table was still dressed up with lovely ware, but standards were not so rigid, especially for waiters and waitresses, whereas bread-and-butter plates were expected and wine was optional. The least demanding of all, Informal tables were set unpretentiously and often invited guests to wait on themselves. When entertaining was buffet-style, equipment, cost, and labor were further reduced.

Today's conditions of rising costs and unavailability of domestic help have increased the prevalence of Formal Buffet settings (formerly, buffets were considered mostly Informal) that incorporate qualities of all three. By combining fine appointments with informal serving of food, those who have valuable tableware or family heirlooms can use them even though they lack household help, or are unable to engage it for a seated dinner.

One of the most important aspects of table setting is its tone, sometimes called spirit or mood. This should be uniform in all appointments and appropriate for the occasion. In general, logic will guide you. For example, if you were planning a dinner-dance on an open patio, you would not use delicate stemware since it might be blown over and broken. Burlap, or similar coarse materials would be unsuitable for making napkins because of irritating the skin even though they matched a cloth. Other illustrations also suggest a common-sense approach. A champagne party, following a symphony concert, set with checked gingham and heavy mugs would seem as incongruous as antique service plates on an informal supper table before a football game. Aside from such extreme situations, there is a wide latitude in table settings that allows you to play down a formal occasion, or dress up an informal one. Within reason, a setting should meet individual needs rather than conform to arbitrary guidelines.

Settings and Rooms   The suggestion is often made that for unity a table setting should reflect the style and color scheme of the dining or living room, if meals are taken there. Sound advice for those with conservative

OLD WORLD INFORMALITY. *A tea table set with pewter and antique Worcester tea plates and cups on grandmother's linen, cut-work cloth, measured to fit the table, reflect the Early American period of the breakfast room. Dusty miller repeats the pewter scheme accented with dark red dahlias and celosia from the garden.* [KLENDER]

QUIET ELEGANCE. *Though the setting is elaborate, including antique Limoges china, point de Venise cloth, ormulu and bronze container and candelabra, appointments enhance rather than compete with each other, each contributing one essential element of color, contrast, texture, or pattern that the others lack. Burnished gold dominates the scheme carried out in the centerpiece by yellow, coral, and orange flowers.* [SPINEK]

tastes, but restricting for others who enjoy experimenting. For example, if your furnishings are modern and in strong colors, as background, they would prevent your using the delicate textures and colors of organdy and Limoges china. If your house is eighteenth-century French, you might feel you should resist vivid place mats and wooden plates. However, though you may prefer to live in one style, sometimes you may want your table to be another, just for fun or for a change. If so, disregard convention, experiment, let your table offer a different picture from that of the room. In other words, enjoy yourself, and no harm done.

Importance of Coordination

When you plan a setting, relate the appointments—glassware, cloth, centerpiece, and other dishes—to the style, color, and texture of the china patterns. Dinner plates by their size and quantity dominate the scheme, whereas the cloth makes a background. If colorful or ornate plates are featured, the rest of the setting should be toned down. Select plainer china for use with embroidered or printed table coverings. Coarse-textured linens go with heavier tableware; finely woven linen, damask, lace, and organdy are reserved for more formal tableware, and the categories are rarely interchangeable.

The size of the table determines the number of settings; its shape and position in the room influence the plan. A square table against a wall in a dinette requires different seating from an oval one in an open central area. Although most settings are symmetrically placed around a centerpiece, an alternate plan could feature matched centerpieces at each end, the guests facing one another across the two sides. But no matter what the design, it should appear balanced.

All the china need not match. If it does, the table is often less distinctive than one that correlates different patterns. Dinner plates should be the same, but an odd set of bread-and-butter or salad plates might be used. Combinations add variety provided there is a unifying characteristic, as a gold-banded edge, a similar design, or related colors. On the other hand, a setting of oddments would hardly appear composed.

When you select different materials, mix only those of the same type. Formal appointments of silver and crystal can accompany fine china, but informal pottery, pewter, wood, copper, and brass rarely relate to elegance. Furthermore, pewter is incompatible with copper or brass because of the difference in finishes. Although stemware is customary for a formal table, good-quality glassware of simple design can be substituted. But avoid mixing traditional and modern elements, as delicate flowers with geometric patterns or straight or angular shapes with those that look rococo.

Keep the setting uncluttered. Don't destroy clean lines by loading

MIX AND MATCH. *Appointments need not match but here the Mexican theme and dominant turquoise hue tie them together. For contrast, asters, celosia, and dahlias in white and shades of red pick up colors in candlestick, container, and cloth.* [KLENDER]

a table with too many nonessentials—compotes, figurines, cigarette holders, ashtrays, decanters, or other items not necessary to a meal (eating). For overall orderliness, place settings squarely, as well as uniformly, one inch from the edge of the table and at an equal distance of at least twenty-four inches from each other.

Centerpieces   Guidelines for table settings may also be applied to centerpieces. Unless colors and textures of plant materials are coordinated with appointments and the design of the arrangement complements that of the table as a whole, the centerpiece will not look appropriate. For centerpieces, first select a container suitable in size, shape, and character, formal or informal according to the setting. Thus, a wicker basket looks better with pottery dishes than silver. Also your bowl or compote should not be so ornate that it vies for attention with the flowers, nor should it be too different from the pattern and color of the china. However, the design may be more effective if a contrasting hue is either featured or incorporated.

For a seated meal, size of table and number of settings determine the proportion and scale of an arrangement. According to standard practice, the arrangement should measure one-third the length of the table. The width of the centerpiece is reduced if the table is narrow and settings numerous. Flowers should never sprawl over into glasses or plates. As a rule, make the arrangement no taller than the length of your arm from elbow to fingertip; otherwise the centerpiece interferes with conversation across the table. Low horizontal designs are favored for a seated meal, although more dramatic effects are achieved when an arrangement is elevated above eye level on a tall candlestick container or compote. (Arrangements for buffet tables will be discussed under that heading later in the chapter.) Proper heights for centerpieces also apply to candles. They should stand either well above or well below eye level to avoid flickering flames in the line of vision. These guidelines also apply to flower shows.

Although plant materials are less well defined today, some varieties and combinations are still considered more formal than others. Easter and calla-lilies are usually appropriate only for an elegant table, but Mid-century lilies could be used for almost any occasion; it would depend on the flowers and foliages with them. Garden roses and snapdragons are not so stiff and uniform in shape as those grown by the florist. Most chrysanthemums appear Informal, but spider chrysanthemums can be Formal or Informal.

As a rule, these materials are considered Informal: most rough-textured foliage including almost all needled evergreen (except in Christmas decorations), ray flowers like asters, dahlias, and mari-golds; spike forms from the garden, such as bells-of-Ireland, celosia, and phlox, also many flowering trees and shrubs, including dog-wood, forsythia, spiraea, and hydrangea. On the list of elegant ma-terials are acacia, anemones, carnations, stock, and many broad-leaved evergreens. Although opinions differ most of the materials not listed here are appropriate for any occasion.

As with the container, the arrangement should repeat at least one of the colors in the setting, although more distinction results if related or contrasting hues are also featured. As a means of unifying a setting, one of the same flowers is used in the arrangement as appears in the floral design of the china. If the china is colorful, it may be wise to select most of the plant material in the hue that appears in the *smallest* quantity in the china.

Using Blue At one time, blue or purple tableclothes and flowers were frowned upon especially by show judges. Black was unthinkable. According to argument, these colors, fading in artificial light, looked dismal. Furthermore, they created holes in a design. Today these opinions are the exception rather than the rule. (Caution is still advised in flower shows.) The right combination of a dark cloth and brightly colored or white accessories with candlelight can make a dramatic setting; indeed blues and purples should not be categorically excluded. Since much of the beautiful old tableware was decorated with cobalt blue, iris, cornflowers, or delphinium are in perfect harmony, worth the same consideration as more brilliant flowers.

FLOWER SHOW SETTINGS

In flower shows, table settings are divided into two broad categories —Functional and Exhibition. Table settings also include sub-classifications of Formal, Semiformal, and Informal as well as Buffet, Tea Tables, and Segments. The schedule designates the classification of the setting, the meal, the number of places, and the size of the table that the show committee will provide. A Functional table is set for eating unlike the Exhibition table that is purely for display with no thought given to the serving of food. Consequently, the Functional table is arranged conventionally but the Exhibition type permits appointments in any position that makes a good design.

Whatever their style, show tables should stress simplicity and restraint, thus eliminating all but essential equipment. The minimum for a Functional seated table includes cloth (or mats), napkins, dinner plates, and water glasses for the stated number of diners, plus the flower arrangement, and candles, if appropriate. Sometimes accessories are allowed. The arrangement with or without candles and accessories is called the Decorative Unit. It may be placed on the table anywhere that it makes the greatest contribution to the setting and should be well-related in character to it. Flatware is absolutely forbidden. Cups and saucers can sometimes replace water glasses, but should not be added to them, for then the table becomes crowded. No food, cut fruit or vegetables, no artificial flowers or foliage are allowed; artificial fruits are permitted only if sanctioned by the schedule.

Candles are usually required on dinner tables but omitted from breakfast settings. For luncheon, they are justified only if the room is poorly lit or the occasion is special, as a wedding. On tea tables they are optional but usual. Although only unused candles are acceptable, rules on burned tips have been eliminated.

Neatness is expected and any deficiency is penalized. The cloth must be spotlessly clean, ironed without creases (except the lengthwise center fold), fitted properly to the table with an even 12 to 18 inches hanging down on all sides. However, allowances are often made by judges if the overhang at the two ends is a little shorter. The folding of the napkin is optional but edges should meet. If you decide to use mats instead of a cloth, check beforehand to determine the condition of the tabletop. Often tables provided in shows are masonite work-tables or the folding aluminum type unsuitable for mats unless the surface is first covered with wood-grain adhesive-backed paper. For this reason, a tablecloth is usually preferable to mats. Coarse table coverings are permitted for formal settings if these are modern in design. Plates and glasses must be in perfect condition, washed and wiped free of smudges and lint, and metal polished unless of antique patina. If dishes are patterned, face them all in the same direction, and stand glasses at equal distances. Take care to display the exact number of place settings specified by the schedule.

Transporting equipment to the show involves less risk if everything is properly packed. Rolling the cloth on a rod or cardboard cylinder and covering it with a plastic dress bag prevents wrinkles and soil. A wicker basket with compartments for wine bottles makes a safe carrier for glasses, which do not then require wrapping. Plates travel best in the zippered cases used for storing china.

As in other competitive classes, design counts most in judging tables, the emphasis being on proportion and scale. Balance is crucial in Buffet tables where it is more difficult to achieve; for seated settings the requirement of symmetry is usually met automatically since a conventional plan is followed. Proportion is determined and evaluated according to the size of the table. The arrangement, candlesticks, and accessories (if any), should be in proportion and scale to it. Show tables are often of different dimensions than standard home tables. Therefore, an arrangement for a seated meal must be proportioned expressly for the size of the table provided at the show; otherwise points will be lost. Trying out your arrangement beforehand on a table of proper size prevents mistakes. Other points of judging tables include harmony, color compatibility, originality, and distinction. These are discussed in Chapter 20.

Although the floral unit is important in the coordination of the setting, it is often judged by itself as a percentage of the total score on the basis of theme interpretation, compatibility, and design. Plant materials are appraised for freshness and grooming, also the mechanics and construction of the arrangement. A centerpiece for a seated meal will be judged from a seated position and should be made from that vantage point. Front and back require the same, or corresponding treatment, if they will be seen from both sides of the table. If viewed from the front only, the arrangement must still be neatly finished in the back.

Buffet Tables in Shows

Buffet settings are by nature different, although the same requirements for coordinating appointments apply. The setting is always functional. Since the purpose of a Buffet table is to encourage self-service, the setting must include two or more serving dishes plus the specified number of plates and glasses or cups and saucers all placed for easy access. Furthermore, the dishes must have a proper relationship to the type of food being served. Thus a coffee pot would not appear with beer mugs, nor a soup tureen accompany salad plates.

Buffet tables are difficult to set because they must look balanced and be Functional as well. When plates that are visually heavy are placed opposite lightweight glasses, one side of the table appears heavier than the other. A scheme must be devised for equalizing them. Napkins, serving dishes, candles, and flower arrangement should be placed where they will strengthen rather than disrupt the rhythm of the design. For example, it would be more convenient if the iced-tea pitcher were next to the glasses, and the casserole near the dinner plates. But then the table could be lopsided with the tall forms all on one side and the low appointments on the other, and a reverse plan restoring balance would create confusion in serving food.

Fortunately, there are no restrictions on the types of serving dishes to be displayed and no definite locations for appointments. This makes Buffet settings a challenge, allowing the exhibitor to experiment with the selection and arrangement of equipment for the most logical as well as the most pleasing design. Plates may be stacked as a unit, spread out, or piled in series of two's or three's (according to the number requested in the schedule), set in the central area of the table or divided in groups at each side. Dishes and glassware are staggered, clustered, or they may form rows or geometric patterns. Napkins too may be placed at will. It is sometimes helpful when arranging a buffet table to think of it as divided into four parts and balance it accordingly.

The floral design is unlimited in height. It may stand wherever it makes the greatest contribution to the design of the setting as a whole. Although proportionate to the size of the Buffet table, the centerpiece is usually taller and more imposing than one for a seated meal, for it must dominate a greater quantity of tableware and will be seen from a standing position. When the arrangement is placed at the rear of the Buffet table, it requires only a frontal design that, nevertheless, should be completed at the back to add depth and finish.

Segment Tables　　Segment tables have been added to the category of table settings to decrease the space requirements for exhibits, to reduce effort and expense for contestants, and to encourage innovative staging. Reminiscent of a still-life, a Segment includes only a single place

A PARTY TO PAINT. *An Exhibition Segment table illustrates a setting suited to still-life or to commercial display. The color scheme of pink, gold, and yellow in flowers and tableware, is attractive with the ecru point de Venise refectory runner and antique satin fabric that doubles as cloth and background.* [ROBINSON]

setting, the linen with napkin, and a decorative unit to suggest a complete table. Sometimes accessories may be used if stated in the schedule. A Segment is similar to a commercial display in effect and purpose. Both attempt to show a creative coordination of colors, textures, and styles while keeping appointments to a minimum.

Although classified according to Functional or Exhibition settings like other table classes, Segments differ in the size and space needed to stage them because there is less equipment. Functional Segments are set in the customary manner for actual use, but they can be displayed on a small table, as a card table, or several entries may be shown on a long table with separate sections for each contestant. A cloth or mat is placed conventionally. The size of an arrangement for a Functional Segment should be scaled to fit *a standard dining table instead of to the dimensions of the space provided at the show*. This distinguishes it from a setting for one; the arrangement in this case scaled to the card table or whatever size space the exhibitor is assigned. The rule for Functional Segments is often confusing, but if you remember to make the floral design approximately one-third the length of a standard table, the centerpiece is likely to fit almost any staging. However, should size need clarification, it is always best to check with the consultant for the class or show chairman as requirements sometimes differ from show to show.

An Exhibition Segment is a departure from the norm. Since it is created primarily as an artistic design without practical considerations, appointments may be staged in any way that promotes distinction. The plate is usually placed perpendicularly on a stand, but its location and its proximity to other appointments are left to the exhibitor to decide. Occasionally, two plates or napkins of different sizes and patterns are shown, or a glass with a cup and saucer, or other accessories may be used if space and schedule permit. To add to their display quality, Exhibition Segments are usually staged against a backdrop that simulates an up-ended table top. Over this,

SMART STYLING OF A CLASSICAL THEME. *In this Exhibition Segment, distinction is the keynote. The decorative unit of dried mullein, bird-of-paradise leaves, sea coral, and gerbera in a compote is raised on a pedestal of alabaster bookends to increase the height to the proportion necessary for the space. Though the scheme is restricted to black, coral, and earthy tones, shades and patterns are sufficiently varied to prevent monotony.* [KLENDER]

the tablecloth can be draped vertically behind the exhibit and also overhang and cover the surface on which the setting stands. Sometimes a paneled wall or other surface with a wood-grain finish is used as background instead of a cloth, which then covers and overhangs the table only. A mat and table runner might be used instead.

The floral composition for an Exhibition Segment should be proportioned to the height of the *exhibition space not to a standard dinner table* like the Functional Segment. It must be tall enough to compensate for the added height of the background. For this reason, a tall, buffet-type centerpiece is usually more suitable than a low design. Should the arrangement lack height to fill the space, it can be elevated on a base or stationed on a platform or box concealed beneath the cloth. Other objects may be similarly raised. Again, it is helpful to practice setting up the exhibit at home, but under flower-show conditions.

The judging of Segment tables follows the same procedure as for other table settings: good design, coordination, skill, and ingenuity are still sought. Interpretation of flower-show themes is also relevant and this is discussed in Chapter 20.

A useful reference is *The Art of Table Setting and Flower Arrangement* by Sylvia Hirsch. Revised 1967, T. Y. Crowell Co.

16

JAPANESE STYLES FOR AMERICANS

Japanese floral art has strongly influenced American flower arrangement. Although Ikebana bears little resemblance to Western massed-line, the principles help to train your eye to recognize design potential in plants and to improve your skill in developing their best features. You can adapt oriental methods and mechanics to almost any design since their theories of balance and proportion have greatly influenced our own work. In fact, proficiency in Japanese styles goes far to develop competence; it also prepares the way for modern design. After you have mastered conventional rules and patterns, put them aside and simply apply the fundamentals.

The character of a people is reflected in its art. Its character reveals attitudes toward life and levels of advancement, as is apparent in Ikebana, which means "living flowers." To the Japanese, their floral art involves their religion and their social structure. Through Ikebana, they idealize nature. Respecting natural growth forms, they improve them by pruning and bending. Through Ikebana they seek to convey the beauty of a landscape, even one lovely flower may symbolize a garden.

Origins The practice of Ikebana goes back to sixth-century China when simple offerings of flowers were placed before Buddha. Ono-no-Imoko, a Japanese scholar who had gone to China to study, brought

EMPHASIZING BEST FEATURES. *Based on Japanese techniques of pruning and theories of proportion and balance, beauty of line has been revealed in this branch of magnolia.* [SUTER]

back Ikebana to his own country. He formulated the rules observed today, and he is credited with founding the earliest school. This is called the Ikenobo School, and the building still stands on the original site. Today Ikenobo remains a prominent influence in Ikebana. The present headmaster is the forty-fifth descendant of the founder.

Although Ikebana emerged in the fifteenth century as a secular art, it was originally taught in the temples by priests, and its study was the prerogative of men. For many years nobles and warriors were the only students; through the practice of Ikebana, they sought to ease the tensions of life by shifting their thoughts from violence to peace. To this day, Ikebana is dominated by men, and it is men who have organized most of some 3000 schools of Japanese arrangement. However, women are now permitted to study as well as to teach, and, since the 1900's, training in the art has become a requirement for women prior to marriage.

Rikka (ree-kah)
Style

Ikebana appeared originally in quite simple design; subsequently it became a formal temple art and was reserved for the privileged class. Under their sponsorship, a style called Rikka was developed on a grand scale, with arrangements 6 to 40 feet high. Since size precluded display in home settings, Rikka was limited to temples and palaces. It required a tremendous amount of material that demanded considerable time and skill to compose. Often several days and a group rather than a single master were needed to produce a Rikka.

Rules for construction were indeed complex and no deviations were permitted. Combinations of materials involved specific categories of woody plants, of grasses, and of flowering plants; symbolic associations determined placements. Branches represented hills and mountains; flowers, plains and valleys; aquatic plants, their own habitat. Even the level of water in a container was significant; in summer it had to be higher than in winter. Many of these rules have endured.

Selection of materials accounts for a major difference between Oriental and Western designs. Whereas we observe principles of harmony, coordinating colors and textures as contrasting or analogous, the Japanese consider this approach artificial. In Ikebana materials are related to the seasons with little regard to color. With us, color must be harmonious. For example, the "Seven Grasses of Autumn," a combination popular in all Ikebana, incorporates pink Chinese bellflowers, bush-clover, kudzu vine, miscanthus (also called eulalia grass), wild morning-glory-vine, patrinia, and eupatorium (some varieties known as Joe-Pye-Weed). For us, the colors —pink, yellow, and purple—do not appear compatible.

The Japanese also endow plants with moods and language. Thus, gerberas suggest sadness; hostas, devotion; hydrangeas, conceit; narcissus, self-love (from the Greek); and pansies, friendship. Sentiments from arranger to recipient are conveyed through materials.

Some combinations are traditional. Plum is masculine and preferred with tulips; plum is associated with pine and bamboo in a New Year's arrangement called "The Three Friends of Winter." Cockscomb goes with evergreens, not with fall foliage since the colors are too close. In the West, yellow celosia and turning leaves become a pleasing analogous scheme.

Such strictures on materials for a Rikka, and often for other styles, were followed by equally rigid patterns of design. All was symbolic, in accordance with ancient Buddhist scriptures. Originally seven branches constituted the framework of a Rikka; the number has since been increased to nine or eleven, plus flowers and leaves. Each part is named, the tallest and most important branch, *shin,* representing a mountain. Other elements, measured and placed at specific angles represent a sunny and a shady side, waterfalls, hills, towns, valleys, and so forth. Thus the height and association of plant materials suggest a landscape. Distance and a third dimension are indicated by the placement of branches and flowers for near and far views. This method of attaining perspective can be applied to Western designs.

Borrowing from Ikebana, we avoid parallel branches, even numbers, and flowers or branches facing down or away from the center of a design. Both East and West favor inserting material at different angles, turning flowers in various directions, and graduating sizes for transition and movement. Rikka, the most massive of Japanese classical styles, does not constitute traditional Western mass arrangement because of its openness and strong linear quality. Yet the apportionment of space relates to our massed-line compositions that are also based on linear pattern, and materials usually share characteristics. In a Rikka, although flowers and foliage are often arbitrarily chosen, any lack of dominance is compensated for by effective use of space that unifies the design.

A Rikka might consist of but one or two materials, but it is not unusual for many materials to be used and all different. Although an assortment avoids monotony, it can fail to provide dominance.

CLASSICAL RIKKA. *Difficult to master, the structure of a Rikka so integrates the parts that the whole resembles a single tree trunk. This design with eleven materials is called Meiji Rikka, a style at least 100 years old. No matter what the top curves or angles of insertion may be, all branches and flower stems meet in the center. Arrangement supervised by Mrs. Toki Miyakawa, Ikenobo professor.* [KLENDER]

Usually the Japanese method of construction takes care of this. Difficult to master, the structure of a Rikka so integrates the parts that the whole resembles a single tree trunk. No matter what the top curves or angles of insertion may be, stems of branches and flowers all meet in the center. In any arrangement, when stems are kept close together (but not packed) on a holder, a disjointed look is avoided. Furthermore, experimenting with various materials develops recognition of characteristics that unify dis-similarities. When executed according to rules, a Rikka is an awesome sight and practically assures an end product of high calibre whether you are artistic or not. What this means is that if you can learn to put a Rikka together through proper measurements and placements, you can create a masterpiece, even though you may be deficient in taste or color sense, for the design is systematized.

The attitude toward balance emphasizes another difference between East and West. Whereas we distribute visual weight, the Japanese rely upon effects that sometimes disturb our sense of equilibrium. Yet their methods are understandable once we realize that orientals rely on nature not principles of design as we do. Since materials are placed as they appear in nature, low-growing plants relate to the container as they do to the ground, regardless of size, and small flowers often appear at the base of a Japanese arrangement beneath bigger forms just as nature has destined them. There they also serve as filler.

For us, such placements look top heavy; we place larger, darker material in the lower areas to provide weight there. Relative positions are further affected because in the East plants are symbols of the sexes. Trees, strong colors, and fully-open buds are associated with the male; grasses and flowers, white and subdued hues and buds are female. Thus materials, regardless of size or hue, take the same positions in a design that people hold in a masculine-oriented society, for the Rikka structure reflects Japanese feudalism, *the shin* a symbol of the dominating sovereign.

IN LINE WITH NATURE. *Adapting the Japanese approach of composing materials as they grow to the Western sense of balance, large tulips are placed in the low central area to give stability at the base of the design where it is needed most.* [SUTER]

In and Yo

In Ikebana, balance is based on the Yin-Yang theory of female-male relationships and this is employed to achieve order. A Rikka representing the cosmos relies on the positive and negative forces of In and Yo, and employs them in unequal amounts. Always at variance, they must be brought into balance. Conforming to ancient Chinese theory, the Japanese In and Yo correspond to the Chinese Yin and Yang and equate the passive female qualities with In and the active male traits with Yo. Thus, the Universe comprises good and evil, darkness and light, weak and strong, left and right. Nature resolves the struggle for supremacy through a balance that permits both to exist.

Ikebana then is based on plant materials endowed with In and Yo attributes. Many plants also have a left and right side, as well as a back and front, depending on which part has faced the sun. Right-hand arrangements, upright forms, and the surface of leaves are male; their opposites, female.

Nageire (na-geh-ee-reh) and Tea Ceremony

Although the Rikka style endured as a revered Ikebana form, especially for religious observances and exhibitions, disadvantages gave rise to other types of arrangement. Styles in art often change when modes of expression no longer fit a society. This is what happened to the classic Rikka style, which was impractical for general use, especially for the middle class, which gained power in the eighteenth century. Moreover, its strict design inhibited creative expression. A more casual style of Ikebana was sought that would be suited to simple home interiors. Thus the Shoka or Seika style developed and this is considered by many to be the apogee of Japanese floral art.

The introduction of the tea ceremony brought an Ikebana form essential to the ritual. Known as *Chabana,* and requiring but a single flower, it was the forerunner of the Nageire or thrown-in style. Nageire depended on the angles at which plant materials came in contact with the base and sides of a tall, narrow vase rather than on artificial positioning devices. Flowers were arranged as if they were growing and so suited the simplicity of Japanese interiors. Henceforth, flower arrangement no longer belonged exclusively to the affluent and the religious hierarchy; Ikebana moved into the home where a place of honor, the tokonoma, a small, stagelike alcove, was created for its display, and this is a standard feature of most Japanese domestic architecture.

In the tokonoma emphasis is placed on an art object, a scroll, a lovely container, and an arrangement. This traditional exhibit, a continual source of pleasure, is changed frequently and always reflects the seasons. Although Nageire is especially suited to the tokonoma, it is also appropriate to any casual, uncluttered setting. Its method of construction has helped Western designers develop techniques of balance.

NAGEIRE INSPIRATION. *The spirit of nageire is retained though the feeling is unmistakably Western in this massed line of flowering branches and roses, but in observance of Japanese rules, the handle of the antique oriental basket remains visible.* [SUTER]

Shoka or Seika
Style

In time the vastly different styles of Rikka and Nagiere were combined to form an in between style that retained the best characteristics of each. The Shoka or Seika style evolved with three of the original Rikka branches used in a Nagiere-type design. Although the basic number of main lines has remained fixed, as are their positions, Shoka style can be varied through the use of auxiliary lines and various combinations of materials, but usually no more than three kinds in a classical design. Essentially asymmetric, Shoka features the union of stems at the base. These are stripped and rise for several inches above the mouth of the container like a single tree trunk or "leg," as the Japanese call it. This union creates a center of interest, the bare stems contrasting with the fullness of flowers and foliage above. The effect is comparable to the Western focal area where all lines converge.

Characteristic of a Shoka is the heaven-man-earth pattern. Strongly linear, featuring graceful curves of branches, Shoka perpetuates a classical style and reflects the oriental preference for asymmetric triangular design. The principle of three that underlies its structure signifies a trinity and can represent Buddha, the Law, and the Priesthood, or male and female in relation to the universe; it depends on whether the interpretation is Buddhist or Shinto.

The heaven-man-earth placements are so fundamental to Ikebana that schedules for Japanese arrangements in American flower shows require not conformance to a particular school, but merely a design that emphasizes three lines in an open triangular pattern. A triangle in some form can be observed in almost all Western compositions, massive or linear. The symmetric and L-shaped versions constitute two standard styles. Traces of a triangle can be found in most others. The Shoka is also responsible for establishing rules of proportion and balance that now apply to all Western designs. The ratio of stem length to container—one-and-one-half times—as well as alignment of the tip of the main line over the center of an arrangement are two practices almost certain to insure proper height and stability.

TRACES OF A TRIANGLE. *Oriental or Western, a triangle underlies most floral composition. Here, design "in the Japanese manner" is guaranteed by the three strong heaven-man-earth lines dividing space in an open pattern.* [SUTER]

By establishing three lines as a frame, the limits of all other materials are fixed.

The universal popularity that greeted the Shoka style has persisted, due to its simplified construction and the opportunities offered for individual expression. Divided into sub-styles, arrangements can be Formal, Semiformal, or Informal. In the East these classifications have different connotations than in the West where designs are also categorized according to their degree of formality. Both Rikka and Shoka are essentially formal in the sense that they follow a conventional pattern. Yet they can differ, not because one is more elegant or casual than another, but through the position and curves of branches. Thus as styles within a style, Rikka and Shoka can be Formal, *shin,* the main branch straight; Semi-formal, *gyo,* the main branch curving; or Informal, *so,* the main branch sweeping. The type of container also indicates the formality of a design; tall, narrow vases for *shin* style, wide-mouthed types for *gyo,* and low or two-tiered vessels for *so.* Arrangements can be either right-handed or left-handed, according to the direction in which the shin or main line curves.

Modern Styles

Shoka perpetuated the classical style; it also was responsible for the rise of modern Ikebana. Heretofore, flower arrangement had been controlled by the Ikenobo School, but the versatility of Shoka stimulated independent interpretation, prompting many masters to break with tradition and set up schools of their own.

Moribana (mor-ee-bah-nah) Style

As Ikebana has made inroads into the West, so the West has influenced the East. Early in the twentieth century, Western culture was introduced to Japan. With it came plants unknown in the East, and attempts were made to incorporate them into oriental floral art. As a result, the Moribana style emerged. An innovative concept of piling up flowers in a low dish was conceived by Unshin Ohara, who founded a school in his name and thus caused a major break with the past. The easy grace of his naturalistic designs constructed with only a simple needle-holder and offering an unlimited choice of materials granted the greatest freedom of any style. Moribana spread quickly. In 1930, a group of masters issued a manifesto entitled, *Declaration of the Newly Risen Style of Flower Arrangement.* In it they denounced the rigidity of classical styles and advocated the use of plant materials without fixed forms as a medium of self-expression.

Sofu Teshigahara was leader of the revolutionaries and founder of the Sogetsu School, which he continues to head. Influenced by the concepts of modern art, he had kept pace with its trends, reflecting them in his arrangements as early as the 1920's. In initiating avant-garde and free-style compositions, Sofu has flouted rules, and, in effect, liberated Japanese floral art. No longer confined to the tokonoma, Ikebana has found a new identity under his leadership, becoming a form of sculpture, taking its place among major arts in public and in the home.

Popular support for the modern movement forced reassessment of strict classical concepts with the result that older schools, their survival threatened, began to update their styles. Even the Ikenobo School introduced a modern Rikka, called Shohin or House Rikka, that has met with great success. Yet the basic tenets of Ikebana were so firmly entrenched that they could not be ignored even by the Sogetsu and Ohara schools. It became evident that competent creative design was not possible without knowledge of principles and techniques. Thus the interchange was complete, the classical schools embracing modern forms, and the innovators relying on the standard patterns of Nagiere and Moribana as fundamental training for avant-garde designing.

For further discussion, see *Japanese Flower Arrangement for American Homes* by Mary Badham Kittel (The Viking Press, Inc., New York, 1962), and *Japanese Flower Arrangement, Classical and Modern,* by Norman Sparnon (Charles E. Tuttle Co., Inc., Tokyo, 1960).

17

FROM TRADITIONAL TO MODERN

At first glance, an occidental and an oriental arrangement side by side seem as far apart as the distance between the two continents—the European composition an opulent mass, the Eastern design restrained, an open linear silhouette. Though the styles are as different as the cultures that produced them, both have had the same inspiration, the love of nature. The simple design reflects the spirit and philosophy of the Japanese, Ikebana symbolizing the beauty of the plant world. In contrast, Europeans, prizing a garden for its abundance and variety, reflect the skill of the gardener in a profusion of materials.

Traditional arrangement in the United States represents the merging of the two attitudes into a massed-line concept which is uniquely our own. This asymmetrical composition, strongly linear in direction is supported by mass that aids and embellishes line but in no way alters it. For example, if the line were an S-curve, subordinate material would broaden it, not draw it away from the established course or confuse the direction. A massed-line arrangement can be composed of a combination of curving branches, spikes, round blooms, and filler, as plum foliage, snapdragons, carnations, and sweet peas; or the design could be limited to a few broader forms that are still linear in shape, as ti leaves and bird-of-paradise flowers.

Although the American style is associated specifically with

massed-line design, since World War II the range has been broadened to include other types. All are now included under the general heading of American Contemporary Arrangement, which has two main divisions: (1) Conventional or Traditional, including Line (showing Japanese influence), Western Massed-Line, and Mass with Period Styles; and (2) Modern, related to the Japanese Sogetsu School of arranging and modern art. Despite its derivation, American design, traditional or modern, unlike its oriental and European parents is based not on nature but on principles of art.

American Conventional Arrangement

Conventional arrangement is the opposite of modern. Mainly decorative, it appeals to the senses—to sight, touch, and smell—and emphasizes natural lines of growth and aesthetic qualities of color, form, and texture. Unconventional patterns and practices are here considered the antithesis of beauty and serenity. Conventional composition stresses smooth transition and harmonious relationship in which similarities predominate over differences introduced as contrast. Graceful rhythm is favored over forceful or conflicting movement; lines converge in a strong center of interest that consolidates them. Forms progress logically in size, colors are graded, and materials are consistent in character. Space is more important around the perimeter than within the body of the arrangement. A traditional design creates a picture that enhances its location, complementing the style and tone of furnishings.

Line Arrangements

Traditional line compositions are usually naturalistic. Inspired by natural forms, they employ materials realistically to produce a scenic interpretation, though not an exact scene. They depend upon normal patterns of growth and existing curves. Flowers and foliage are pruned to clarify line and accentuate, not distort, natural characteristics. Similarity of material is preferred.

Traditional line arrangements are simple and clean cut, usually asymmetrical in a spacious open pattern of few materials. Although round flowers may comprise the focal area, they are placed in a linear pattern and not massed. Little if any filler is used. If a line design does not carry enough visual weight, a delicate main line may be strengthened by increasing its length beyond the standard proportions of materials to container. In a flower-show class with a line theme, any arrangement in which secondary material adds mass is disqualified, since the result would then be more typical of massed-line than pure line. Of all designs, line is the most rhythmic.

Massed-line Arrangement

In character, a massed-line arrangement is closer to mass than line though the linear quality predominates. Arrangements are usually full, composed of a quantity of material of similar character. Combinations feature related colors and textures with some contrasts. Composition is based on continuity with transitional materials permitting change to take place gradually. The strongest part of the design is through the center, since balance and symmetry originate from a central axis; and materials with the most prominent characteristics are placed there to draw attention to the area. Pleasing outline and orderly arrangement of materials, placed to emphasize depth, are typical aspects of massed-line composition. Of all styles, this one is probably the best suited to most American homes.

Mass Arrangement

Mass arrangements are of broad dimension and contain a quantity of homogeneous materials that radiate from a central point. They derive from seventeenth- and eighteenth-century flower paintings. Mass designs are usually round, oval, triangular, or fan-shaped within a closed silhouette. Flowers and foliage can be either loosely arranged in an airy bouquet similar to French eighteenth-century styles, or more tightly organized but not crowded in the Victorian manner. Other characteristics typical of massed-line and traditional composition apply except for the absence of perceptible linear direction. Instead, design depends on materials grouped by kind to create a pattern.

When Is Mass Line, and Line Mass? *Here, mass supports line (massed-line) merging with it but in no way altering its course; the arrangement includes buddleia, zinnias, and andromeda berries.* [SUTER]

Period Design as Reference

Period arrangement, the source of mass, is studied as an aspect of it, the subject encompassing a range of styles that parallel trends in art. Although the earliest forms of floral decoration were not mass, they nevertheless mark the beginning of period styles and are, therefore, essential to their history. Some of the best known of these styles of later periods are impractical because they require a quantity of materials that is expensive and difficult to compose. However,

FULL-BODIED. *This is pure mass in quantity, dimension, silhouette, and total absence of perceptible line.* [SUTER]

they provide a reliable source for study and suggest patterns worth simplifying for our more modest needs.

Period arrangements document styles in design, accessories, containers, and colors that were fashionable in a country of leading influence, as Georgian in England in the eighteenth century. Plant materials are those that were known during the era that the composition represents.

When you compete in a flower-show class requiring an *authentic* period arrangement, consult documented illustrations to insure accuracy. The inclusion of flowers, especially hybrids, unknown during the time depicted, or containers of atypical material may result in disqualification, although substitutions approximating original types, when these are not available, are often permitted. For instance, chrysanthemums would not be allowed in a seventeenth-century Flemish arrangement as this flower was not introduced from China until about 1764. On the other hand, if you did not have a silver urn for a Georgian composition, a lusterware ceramic of recent manufacture might be acceptable if the shape were correct.

Since European painting and decorative arts offer the principle examples of early flower compositions, we turn to the history of Western art as background for the styles that influenced our traditional designs in general and mass arrangement in particular.

Art as Reference   The development of floral design from antiquity until the late nineteenth century is found in paintings and artifacts. Surviving classical pottery illustrates the Greek and Roman stylized patterns that followed the shape of the vessels. Murals show wreaths and garlands used in religious and athletic ceremonies. Laurel and other foliage twisted in circles with nuts, cones, or berries have inspired similar designs today, and they were the forerunner of the Della Robbia wreaths of the sixteenth century. Perhaps our traditional fruit and vegetable harvest compositions can also be attributed to the Roman way of massing fruits and flowers in baskets and cornucopias, containers we still use.

During the Middle Ages, frescoes, mosaics, and tapestries displayed included plant materials in natural scenes. The earliest examples of vase flowers appeared in fifteenth-century oil paintings

Two in One. *Though not conforming exactly to a period, this lavish display of fresh flowers in copies of French antique vases is noticeably period-influenced.* [KLENDER]

where the flowers were incidental symbols in large religious works. A rose or a lily might be casually placed in a simple receptacle beside the Virgin to represent her virtues of love and chastity.

As the Middle Ages merged into the Renaissance toward the middle of the fifteenth century, nonreligious art became important, and in the late sixteenth century, the discovery by the Dutchman Zacharias Janssen of the principle of the microscope and the magnifying glass made possible close examination of plants. At the same time the introduction of exotic specimens from the East and West Indies, Mexico, and Turkey stimulated interest in botany.

By this course we come to the still-life paintings of the seventeenth-century Flemish school. By including a great variety of plants, an artist could provide himself with many different forms, textures, and colors and so immortalize on canvas the transient beauty of flowers. Compositions produced from this time until the middle of the nineteenth century, when an interest in floral subjects waned, furnish the models for most of our period arrangements today. When flower painting revived in the second half of the nineteenth century, the new masters were Impressionists and they used blossoms and leaves to study the affect of light on color. In the schools that followed, modern art moved farther and farther away from naturalism and another category was added to flower arangement.

CHARACTERISTICS OF PERIOD ARRANGEMENT

Renaissance, Late Sixteenth Century

Floral designs of the Renaissance featured contrasting colors based on triadic harmonies. Uncluttered and pyramidal in shape, arrangements often equalled the height of the container, which might be a classical vase, bowl, jug, or goblet of metal, glass, or pottery. Combinations of dried with fresh plant material were not uncommon, the flowers including anemones, carnations, iris, lilies, and roses. Velvet, brocade, damask, or gold cloth were used as backgrounds.

Baroque Flemish
School,
Seventeenth
Century

Though the Baroque style in Italy dominated in the seventeenth century, most of the well-known flower painters were Flemish or Dutch. Compositions were truly mass, bulging with a quantity of flowers and fruits. More than one center of interest was common and more than one accessory was often displayed at the base, as a stuffed fowl, a bird's nest with eggs, insects, butterflies, a wine decanter, a loaf of bread with a knife, a basket of yarn, even a skull. Oval designs in jewel colors were composed of carnations, celosia, dahlias, foxgloves, peonies, poppies, and parrot tulips and these often spilled over the rim of the container.

Such paintings are breathtaking, but the difficulty that composing such a vast array of materials into a workable design and the mechanics that such construction would require have made me doubt if these arrangements were ever made. I suspect that this floral art belonged to the painter not to the arranger. With a brush it is easy to produce technical wonders impossible in practice. In a painting, stems can be unnaturally curved or straightened in defiance of nature; odd angles of insertion can be contrived, and improbable balance stabilized.

The theory that the seventeenth-century artist may not have painted actual arrangements, merely his concept of them, is supported by the appearance together of flowers from different seasons. Examining one such painting, I counted some two hundred flowers of forty species that certainly did not bloom at the same time. Very likely the artist made sketches when blossoms were available and so built a file for reference. With this system, a still life could be composed at any time of year. Such paintings indicate the styles of the period as well as the years when certain plants were known. Sometimes one flower was made important through exaggeration of its natural height or size. Perhaps this was done to indicate the value of a particular plant, its costliness, rarity or recent introduction from a foreign land. To the artist, a flower might have other than botanical implications, symbolizing instead, a new pigment, a curious form, or a recently introduced hybrid.

French Rococo, Eighteenth Century

In France art changed from the grandiose Baroque style to graceful rococo elegance. Favorite colors changed from gold, deep blue, rouge and putty to the pastels preferred by the Marquise de Pompadour and later Queen Marie Antoinette. Flowers were loosely grouped in asymmetric oval designs without centers of interest. Branches might be two to three times the height of a container. Earlier favorite flowers were supplemented by delphinium and lilacs as well as acacia, fuchsia, pansies, and violets. These were placed in compotes, baskets, epergnes, jardinieres, vases, or urns of Chinese, Dresden, or Sèvres porcelain, or in bisque, crystal, bronze, silver, or alabaster vessels. Figurines, boxes, fans, or masks often complemented these designs, which were set off against patterned silks, satins, velvets, or tapestries. The S-curve originated at this time by the eighteenth-century English painter Hogarth has become a standard design for arrangements.

French Neo-classicism, Late Eighteenth and Early Nineteenth Centuries

In the second half of the eighteenth century, the tenor of art changed as a result of the fall of Louis XVI and the French court, and there was a reaction against the extravagance of the earlier period. Following the excavations at Herculaneum and Pompeii, interest revived in the classical world and flower arrangement changed, the formal balance of triangular mass replacing curved asymmetry. Colors reflected Napoleon's preference for red, green, white, gold, yellow, and purple.

Georgian, Eighteenth Century

Georgian, the English style that prevailed during the reigns of George I, II, and III, is characterized by stately, symmetrical, and triangular arrangements. Trends set by Wedgwood, Adam, and Chippendale inspired tall, slender compositions in one of three

PROFUSION. *In Victorian splendor, a richly decorated authentic vase overflows with a wealth of fresh flowers.* [KLENDER]

palettes—all-white, variations of one hue, or white contrasted with warm tones. Wine coolers and tureens were used as containers, chintz and crewel work appeared as backgrounds for arrangements of Queen-Anne's-lace, salvia, baby's-breath, and gladiolus. Stafford-shire and Capo-di-Monte pottery and porcelain were favored and accessories included medallions and statuettes, Chinese horses, candlesticks and candelabra, mirrors, and samplers.

Victorian,
Nineteenth
Century

As the middle class rose in power, art and arrangements declined. The nineteenth-century Victorian style is associated with stuffed ornate designs without dominance or centers of interest. Artificial, fresh, and dried plant materials in strong colors were crowded into circular compositions, wider than tall, but shorter than their elaborate containers. Of these, footed trumpet vases encrusted with gold were the most popular, but glass—pressed, blown, milk, hobnail, cranberry—silver, Parian ware and other ceramics, were also in vogue. With such accessories as daguerreotypes, valentines, portrait busts, mother-of-pearl inlaid objects, blackamoor figures, and papier-mâché work, arrangements were staged against backgrounds of plush, velvet, horsehair, and figured wallpaper.

Later in the period, design continued to deteriorate. Containers became heavier and more elaborate, arrangements already glutted were crammed with beaded materials, seashells, and feathers, the whole suffocating under glass domes.

Early American
Colonial,
Seventeenth
Century

American flower arrangement emerged in the seventeenth century. Reflecting the hardships of life, simple mixed bouquets of herbs and flowers generally in warm tones were enjoyed in such household utensils as kettles, bean pots, wooden bowls, glass bottles, and bark baskets. Homespun, chintz, embroidery, and India print fabrics complemented plant materials that included goldenrod, asters, black-eyed Susan, canna, sunflowers, pansy, everlastings, and gourds.

Late Colonial,
Eighteenth
Century

The American floral design in the eighteenth century is sometimes known as Colonial Williamsburg. Since there are no paintings or records to substantiate styles, printed textiles offer the best source of patterns. Arrangements were fan-shaped or triangular, the plant material concentrated toward the rim of the container, sometimes concealing it. Fresh and dried flowers and foliages were rarely combined. However, fruits and flowers might be placed as accompaniment on a table. Arrangements were from one to four or five times taller than containers. These included low bowls, epergnes, cornucopias, and cachepots, "bricks" with holes, wall pockets, and finger vases. Sometimes an elaborate covered vase was used as an accessory. Although muted blues and greens are most characteristic of the Williamsburg arrangements, pastels and deeper hues were also popular.

Federal, Late Eighteenth and Early Nineteenth Centuries

After the American Revolution, French Directoire influences prevailed. Martha and George Washington were innovators, the First Lady introducing formal flower arrangement, the President, new plants from abroad. Reflecting French Empire styles, American adaptations, though still traditionally mass, became thinner and taller with symmetrical balance. The Classic Revival brought a preference for cake baskets, urns, oval vases, and low-footed bowls in glass, silver, and porcelain. Harmonious rather than contrasting color schemes were favored.

In the twentieth century, American floral design changed so drastically that a chapter is devoted to its study.

Since period arrangement is such a big subject, I can only touch on it here. For further study, consult *A History of Flower Arrangement* (revised edition), 1968 by Julia S. Berrall (The Viking Press, Inc.); *Outlines of Period Flower Arrangement* by Frances J. Hannay (National Council of Books, Inc.), 1948 and *Period Flower Arrangement* by Margaret Fairbanks Marcus (M. Barrows & Co., Inc.), 1952. This last is out of print but usually available in libraries.

AMERICAN HERITAGE. *This late colonial room, furnished now as it would have been then, is decorated with a triangular arrangement that spills over the rim of an eighteenth-century Spode basket and tray. Harbre de Venture Room, circa 1762, Baltimore Museum of Art.* [SUTER]

AMERICAN HERITAGE. *Another view with a Chippendale, block-front desk, 1770. Portrait attributed to John Hesselius.* [SUTER]

18

MODERN AND BEYOND

In the same way that art had influenced traditional arrangement, it has set the course for modern design and, in some instances, determined its forms. Once a break had been made with conventional style, both art and flower arrangement moved toward abstraction. The change in art followed the work of the Impressionists and was led by the Postimpressionist Paul Cézanne. He simplified familiar objects into geometric shapes—the cone, the cylinder, and the sphere. Apples became circles, houses squares. Though identity was recognizable, it was not realistic. Credited with founding modern art, Cézanne provided the stimulus for further distortion as succeeding movements in art, beginning with Cubism, became less and less representational. Abstraction was finally reached by the painters, Kandinsky and Mondrian, who were concerned with lines and shapes, colors and textures as elements for patterns of pure design. In this nonobjective art, reality disappeared.

Modern art, a product of the times, reflects political and social unrest. Scientific progress has caused a reassessment of values. The schools of art reacted differently to events, with individual attitudes and judgments.

Futurism chose the machine as a symbol of achievement and employed design to extol the virtues of movement and speed; Dadaism rebelled against the establishment and in attempting to sabotage it created art out of junk; Surrealism was preoccupied with the workings of the subconscious, painting fantasies and dreams to disturb rational thinking; Constructivism adopted new materials and forms, changing the mediums of sculpture to plastics and wires, and its forms from natural to geometric figures.

Influences of Art   New directions in art produced new concepts in flower arrangement. Plant material became a medium similar to paint and clay and was used to express abstract qualities of form, color, and texture rather than botanical associations. It did not matter whether a leaf was yucca or begonia, but whether a rough, gray-green dagger shape expressed an idea better than a jeweled star form. If Piet Mondrian could reduce a tree to a network of vertical and horizontal lines lively with movement, an arranger could achieve such an effect by forcing stems into unnatural positions or distorting the identity of plants through techniques of bending, clipping, knotting, or twisting.

UP-TO-DATE. *Like sculpture, flower arrangement finds in technological materials a medium suited to its art form. Here, a construction of Plexiglas tubes encircled with "bracelets" could function either as container or alone as pure design.* [SUTER]

As technological materials had intrigued artists, these also found their way into floral compositions assuming an importance on a par with flowers and foliage. Copper tubing, Plexiglas, screening, wrought iron brought distinction to design and enlarged its scope.

Space came into its own. Henry Moore had demonstrated how space and form could be interwoven, each with definite shape. Though one had tangible substance, the other gave the illusion of it. Moore treated form as positive volume; space was no longer emptiness; it was negative volume. He brought space into sculpture by hollowing out solid matter, by carving windows in mass, by surrounding air with structure. Floral designers came to employ form and space in the same way; a flower or leaf represented positive volume, space became negative volume, an actual shape when outlined with vines, encircled with branches, or an opening cut in a figure of driftwood. Composition now was designed *with* space as well as in it.

Modern architecture played a key role, too. Under the influence of the German Bauhaus school, the concept of building was revolutionized and the character of interiors and exteriors greatly altered. Conventional solutions to problems of construction were no longer respected. Functionalism became the objective, replacing ornamentation as the effective means of fitting plan to purpose, providing maximum efficiency in the process. Design and structure were one, each essential to the other. Interiors were stark, featuring open space, plain surfaces, clean lines, neutral or strong colors, and simple furnishings. In such settings, traditional floral composition was inappropriate. It required updating and thus took on the characteristics of the environment it was to decorate.

The Assemblage   Of all influences, the "junk art" of the Dadaists was probably responsible for the greatest change by moving flower arrangement toward the assemblage. Who can forget the canoe paddle that substituted for the gladiolus as main line, the sewer pipe as container, or the undulating aluminum clothes lines for rhythm. Anything was fair game. Refrigerators lost their shelves, bathtubs their feet, automobiles their air-filters. Husbands returned home to find basements littered with "treasures" from dumps, and children were surprised to find bicycle seats missing. In one flower show, a contestant won a blue ribbon for a set of golf clubs with a few wilted daisies tied to the tops. Floral art became confused with sensationalism and good taste was forsaken. Chaos had evolved from order.

The new movement was part of an avant-garde style, referred to as Creativity in garden club circles. Its roots lay in the Readymades of Marcel Duchamp. These were ordinary objects, an ironing board or bottle drying rack elevated to the status of art because Duchamp had signed his name to them. It was his purpose to prove that anything made by man or man's machine was art, the artist functioning only as authentication for them. Since these pranks were successful and such works did, in fact, become collectors' items with high price tags, Duchamp made his point; in so doing, he forced a reassessment of what constitutes art with common objects seen in new perspective. He also caused a reclamation of discards whose damaged shapes, deteriorating finishes, and fading colors were now considered to have artistic merit. (Today, we would probably call him an environmentalist.)

One of the basic reasons for the rise of the sculptural assemblage is summed up by Edmund Burke Feldman of the University of Georgia in his book, *Art as Image and Idea* (Prentice-Hall, Inc., Englewood Cliffs, New Jersey, 1967). He points out the inadequacy a sculptor feels when confronted by the forms and fabrication of industrial production. "There is a certain practical wisdom on the part of the sculptor who takes possession of these resources by incorporating products (usually worn out) of industry into his work. His creative strategy shifts from an emphasis on forming skills to an emphasis on ideas and composition, which is to say on design." These remarks are relevant to flower arrangement. Anyone in-

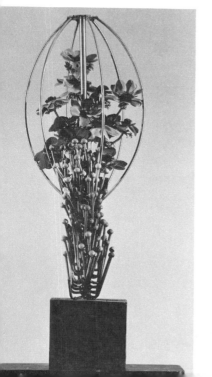

JUNK OR ART? *In this assemblage, found objects, properly associated, make a unique and artistic composition. A giant eggbeater, reappraised as a pattern of curved lines and oval spaces, encloses fresh anemones that burst from a heap of scrap iron salvaged from a demolition site.* [KLENDER]

terested in developing the art of the assemblage should also study the "merz [litter] constructions" of Kurt Schwitters to discover how unusual forms can be related in the building of an abstract design.

My first experience with the assemblage came with a symposium in 1964 sponsored by the Federated Garden Clubs of Maryland. As a participant, I was asked to make one of these new designs which was to be judged as part of the program. Since I had never heard of an assemblage, the chairman of exhibits explained it to me as "a collection of bizarre, unrelated materials, fitted together as a unit." She suggested as one combination, an old bedspring, a piano leg, and a broken toilet seat with some plant material, a blossom or two or just one leaf to qualify the design as a flower arrangement.

I hunted in my cellar as a likely place of inspiration. There I found the lid of a garbage can to use for a base; I painted it black, one of the "in" colors then. My worn-out washing machine, await-ing pickup, offered the agitator for the body of my composition. To elevate it to a proper height for the 42-inch panel assigned me as background, I chose a chipped spice rack spruced up with copper paint. For line, my roofer contributed a drain spout that he had just replaced; the plumber cooperated with a spare toilet float (but my husband appropriated this to replace a faulty one in his office), and the hardware store loaned me the crowning glory, three leaf strain-ers. These excited me for their artistic configurations incorporating space, which was then beginning to assume tremendous importance in design. To comply with the rules, I included a dried wisteria vine and two giant shaggy orange dahlias, the stems stripped of leaves. My creation was stunning. However, it met mixed reactions in the audience, but that was to be expected since most were traditionalists. Nevertheless, my effort won acceptance nationally and was chosen to represent the New Year in the 1965 flower arrangement calendar, *Vision of Beauty* of The National Council of State Garden Clubs, the first assemblage, I believe, they ever published.

*Influence of Sofu
Teshigahara*

Much of the credit for the development of avant-garde arrangement in this country, as well as in Europe, belongs to Sofu Teshigahara. If anyone could recognize design potential, here was the man. To him, the so-called ugly side of nature—withered, dead, diseased, and misshapen materials—deserved as much consideration, if not more, than plants at peak of beauty and freshness. He saw stems as lines of action moving the eye from one point to another, and he employed them bare—this unheard-of before. Thorny branches, long rejected as unsightly, he found valuable for their strange configurations, practically the thorns protected the plant, but artistically they added to its character. Coconut palm, previously relegated to utilitarian broom making, achieved decorative status in his hands. He gave leaves importance over flowers, standing them straight and tall to give dignity. He transformed blooms into mass by compacting them, expanding size by increasing number. In his own words, Sofu sought not to imitate nature but to recompose it.

He realized the importance of space: it separated forms. As he captured more and more space within his compositions, Sofu also saw it as releasing size to greater dimensions. Soon the sky was the limit. His outdoor floral sculptures grew to giant proportions; the tallest, 150 feet, required a team of workers on ladders to construct it, as did many of his other works. Consistently the innovator, he was the first to use driftwood, the first to omit containers, the first to display planter material out of water. Sometimes he has even taken to dispensing with pinholders, nailing thick stems of flowers and vines onto his large constructions. He has shown us how to unify strong contrasts, stating that, "One of my fashions is to fuse two different things in a single piece in an effort to stress individual characteristics of component parts." Manipulating line and form for effect, Sofu is the master of materials, subjecting them to his will.

In turning to metals and other inorganic materials for arrangements, Sofu was prompted more by necessity than by plan. In the war, bombing had destroyed the land, replacing plant life with the raw materials of broken machinery, demolished buildings, and burned tree trunks. Sofu assembled these "found" objects into large-scale abstract and free-form structures. Thus his avant-garde style reflected the conflict that produced it. In this country his ideas were disseminated by army wives who had studied in the Sogetsu School before returning from Japan. Then in 1959, Sofu held a one-man show in the United States, introducing his advanced work at the Martha Jackson Gallery in New York.

Modern Design   Although avant-garde techniques did not emerge in this country until the 1960's following Sofu's lead, modern style in the West originated much earlier. Arrangements, termed "modernistic," were distinguished by stylized, sparse, clean-cut patterns. Reference to them may be found in out-of-print books like *New Flower Arrangement* by Mrs. Walter R. Hine (Charles Scribner's Sons), and *Modernistic Flower Arranging* by Barbara Sagel Meisse (Orange Judd Publishing Co., Inc.), both published in the mid-1930's.

Modern design became an accepted American style in connection with Creativity and these went hand-in-hand with the avant-garde. Creativity was developed as a concept of the National Council of State Garden Clubs to encourage originality in flower shows. Though many disapproved of the new trend and few understood it, Creativity caught on, perhaps because the arrangements looked easy. As opposed to traditional forms requiring quantities of flowers and foliage that were often difficult to organize, modern design required only a few elements and these not restricted to plants. Furthermore, no one seemed to bother about rules, now considered inhibiting to imagination.

Many of these early "creative" designs I called "stick arrangements," because they literally consisted of sticks, and "sticking" them about constituted the chief method of composition. However, in fairness to these early attempts, it must be admitted that the new concepts were confusing. They seemed to contradict accepted standards even though it was claimed that these prevailed as before. Arrangers and judges were still expected to be guided by the elements and principles of design, for these remained constant; it was only the interpretation that was different. But how to reconcile space as form, harmony strengthened by discord, balance sustained by instability, composition devoid of transition and centers of interest, variety overpowering dominance, and unity without relationships? Why contort natural curves as if they were in convulsion or destroy flowers through mutilation? Clearly, more rational directives were needed if order was to be restored. And these were forthcoming.

In due course, modern style became an independent division of Western arrangement with distinctive features as a whole, but with several divisions, as abstract, free style, assemblage, each unique in character. However, all modern arrangements generally share these characteristics:

1. Dynamic balance
2. Abrupt changes
3. Intense, sometimes clashing colors
4. Sharp contrasts
5. Bold forms
6. Clarity of line
7. Few materials
8. Forceful movement
9. Pronounced patterns
10. Exaggerated proportions
11. Imposing sizes
12. Heavy textures, coarse or shiny
13. Exotic material, mostly tropical—anthurium, bird-of-paradise, ginger; large, broad leaves; or common materials employed in unusual ways

Although construction still relies upon line and mass, these are broken up by space and may be composed of other than plant material, though a minimum is required. As a further deviation, the container may predominate and mechanics need not be hidden provided they are integrated through color. More often a base supports a design, to which it may be attached, less often enhances a container, since then it is likely to add weight and interfere with spaciousness. As a whole, modern arrangements are stark, exciting, dramatic, fast-paced, everything a traditional composition is not.

DIVISIONS OF MODERN

Abstract

All abstract designs are modern, but all modern designs are not necessarily abstract. There are also degrees of abstraction, depending on how far a subject departs from reality, or, indeed, suggests it at all. Whereas some abstractions show signs of the original point-of-departure, a nonobjective composition makes no reference to persons, places, or things; design is exploited purely for design's sake. Although this is more easily accomplished in painting and sculpture, *total* abstraction is rarely achieved in flower arrangement since some aspect of the natural material nearly always remains. In character, abstract design is subjective, provoking an emotional reaction. In art, titles that were once descriptive now give no clue to the subject; the viewer must interpret for himself. Paintings of this type are usually difficult to ignore; a spectator experiences either positive or negative feelings, but is rarely unmoved.

The difference between a modern and an abstract flower arrangement rests on composition more than on any other factor. Modern is usually constructed in relation to a strong central core, with stems arising from a common source such as a container, and definite focal areas located in the path of the main line. In many ways structure is the same as in traditional design, even though characteristics are entirely different. An abstract work, on the other hand, is an overall pattern with depth and space, surface and solid of equal value. Materials do not emerge from a single point, nor does a central feature exist to draw the eye to the heart of a design. Instead, each

MORE MODERN THAN ABSTRACT. *In a design that springs from a central source, plastic hose (from an underground sprinkling system) and rectangles convert space to negative volume by defining it and thinly veiling it behind a transparent surface.* [KLENDER]

MORE ABSTRACT THAN MODERN. *An iron construction, dried giant alliums, and fresh tropical ginger become lines, forms, and interposing spaces in a design of continuing movement that has no real beginning or end.* [SUTER]

part is a continuing force but necessary to the whole. This system of composition, known as "plastic organization," underlies abstract design.

Free Style   As the name implies, Free Style arrangements do not conform to established patterns as triangles, ovals, etc. Though still conforming to standard principles, designs are less contained, less ordered, more abstract. At liberty to follow the natural lines of plant materials, the arranger displays greater individuality.

The style originated in the Japanese Sogetsu School as a phase of advanced work in which composition was released from prescribed measurements, placements and rules as incentive to creativity. Any material was permitted, if artistic. Directions for Japanese Free Style cannot be found in any official manual, since guidelines would defeat the purpose. However, though the three standard placements of heaven-man-earth are no longer well-defined, they are nevertheless sensed.

Free Form Although Free Form is similar to Free Style, there is a distinction. All Free Style designs are not by nature Free Form, though a composition that is Free Form is likely to be Free Style. Free Form can be compared to the appearance of water spilled on a table, or better still, to an amoeba. These one-celled animals that we studied under a microscope in high school biology are remembered for their changing shape as a result of reproduction by division and movement through protrusion in various directions. They do not produce a geometric outline, rather an irregular curving outline. Such living organisms influenced the work of the sculptor, Jean (Hans) Arp, who based many of his designs on biomorphic order, the resemblance to biological forms. A Free Form arrangement should reflect the character of amoebic shape, with straight lines restricted to a minimum so as not to disrupt the easy flow.

Collage Collage, introduced by the Cubists, had considerable effect on painting. Forerunner of the Assemblage, Collage resembles a bas relief, since fragments of extraneous material attached to the canvas alter its surface. Pablo Picasso conceived the art in 1912 when he fastened to a still life a scrap of oilcloth, printed to look like chair caning. Georges Braque and Juan Gris, experimented with pieces of newsprint, broken mirrors, and photographs. Depth of design increased as bits of wood, metal, buttons, rope, etc., were added to raise the surface of the painting.

Though the Collage is a concept of abstract art, flower arrangers have been employing a similar technique in traditional wall plaques, nuts, cones, and various dried materials glued to a flat surface. The reason these do not qualify as true collages is that they are conventional by nature consisting of related materials, their similarities more pronounced than their differences. Traditional plaques are an antithesis to abstract floral collages, also fastened to a wood or similar backing, but comprising diverse natural and man-made parts that are not usually associated. In such designs, textural contrasts are dominant with variety unified by an integrating element.

Assemblage Assemblages, discussed above, are mentioned here as a logical outgrowth of collage. Although the two are comparable, an assemblage, a composition of diverse parts, usually more closely approximates free-standing, three-dimensional sculpture.

Mobiles Movement through line has always been implied in art, but Alexander Calder of the Constructivist School and inventor of the mobile, actually set sculpture in motion by employing kinetic energy. In most of Calder's mobiles, movement occurs in response to air currents. Structures are suspended in delicate balance, their light-weight parts connected to turn freely. Plant materials, especially dried ones, are suited to such construction, and even when small moisture-holding mechanics as Oasis or water picks are required for fresh blossoms or leaves, the few extra ounces make little difference.

The principles essential to the design of a mobile are first, balance; without it movement is hindered; and second, repetition or dominance that unifies composition. By nature, a mobile is constructed in a series of parts set far enough apart to prevent bumping or blocking. Spaces increase visual movement as the eye searches for resting places. In Calder's mobiles, repetition of form, size, and color unifies design compensating for separations that could otherwise disrupt it. The charm of a mobile lies in the unpredictably changing patterns.

Artificial Kinetics

Motion may also be produced by an electric or battery-driven motor. The difference in effect between natural and artificial motion has been neatly summed up by Mr. Feldman. "In general, artificial energy causes regular rhythms, recurrent events, intentional motions, whereas the unpredictable and irregular character of natural energy imparts some of its random quality to the sculpture it animates."

For its ease of operation in turning a free-standing design, a turntable is more widely employed in flower arrangement than other types of motorized equipment. (Turntables are sold according to size and capacity for supporting weight.) A rotating arrangement is most effective if lines bend or intertwine to suggest actual motion as angles of viewing change. Motorized effect is related to Op art, which though stationary, employs shifting patterns to produce an optical illusion of movement. Backgrounds of fabric or decorative paper printed with op or psychedelic patterns also suggest motion in an arrangement.

Including a motor within a composition is another source of energy whereby an entire unit or only part of it is activated. A motor may operate by electricity or battery though motors with batteries are difficult to obtain. If you buy an electric motor, select one that runs on house current (110 volts alternating current) and is of suitable gearing and sufficient power or force (torque) to move the weight of your design at the necessary speed. Motors are available in sizes as small as one or two cubic inches and turn as slowly as one or two r.p.m. (revolutions per minute). To connect an arrangement, attach it to the shaft of the motor with a set-screw.

KINETIC MOVEMENT. *Swirling "ribbons" of Plexiglas personify motion whether motionless or revolving as here on a turntable. (The blur is due to motion.) Sculpture by Claire S. Neuman.* [SUTER]

Take care to keep the motor from contact with water even if it is battery-driven.

Most motors sold in hobby shops operate at higher speed than desirable for arrangements and would require gearing-down—a complicated mechanical alteration. Sometimes suitable motors can be obtained free after they have been used in advertising displays for paint or liquor. Other possible sources include repair and supply houses for electric motors, or shops dealing in plumbing equipment or rental enterprises. Of course, if you (or your husband) are mechanically inclined, you can follow the lead of artists and make your own motor.

Stabiles   Stabiles are another Calder innovation. Although a stabile is a stationary sculpture, it appears to move through forceful lines that create the effect of action and arouse a kinetic response. Plant material lends itself to this type of composition since the quality of movement is inherent in natural growth. Even when fixed, branches seem poised, ready to sway or bend, receptive to the slightest stimulus, gentle breeze or a strong wind. Thus a tree symbolizes a stabile.

When parts actually move, they constitute a different structural type, one with a fixed base but moving parts. In "Constellations," Calder combines the principles of stabile and mobile. Though both were originated by Calder, the terms were coined by Arp and Duchamp.

The course of flower arrangement has reached a stage where, as Helen Van Pelt Wilson, my illustrious editor, says in her book, *Flowers, Space, and Motion* (Simon and Schuster, 1971), "The art now faces in two directions . . . the private face is toward the home, its purpose to decorate, but in new ways; the public face is toward the exhibition hall, its purpose to design in the contemporary styles of the other arts, notably sculpture." She captured the essence of modern design when she said, "It represents where flower arrangement is going rather than where it has come from."

19
ARRANGEMENTS IN A NEW LIGHT

The fascination of light has prompted arrangers to explore the possibilities of illumination on arrangements. Although dramatic effects are usually sought, artificial light has other advantages. For example, you can create an artistic picture by simulating natural environment; sunshine, moonlight, or haze each produce a different association. By suggesting atmosphere, you add realism to a theme. Orange and yellow flowers become more vibrant under red and amber lights that also connote a bright day; blue illumination casts a nocturnal glow over the soft gray tones of driftwood, perhaps contributing the illusion of an eerie night.

Light enriches textures, especially on table settings, bringing sparkle to appointments. Light enhances the form and modeling of objects, produces silhouettes, highlights, and shadows. It sets a mood, clarifies details, intensifies contrasts and colors, altering them by distortion, brightening or graying them. Depth is increased by lighting, movement suggested by blinking or flashing lights. In general, light is decorative, softening or sharpening images.

As Silhouette Employing light effectively was illustrated in a state flower show, "Arts and Flowers," sponsored by the Federated Garden Clubs of Maryland. The exhibit won the 1970 Gold Rosette, an award of the National Council of State Garden Clubs. As co-chairman of

THE MOON IS FULL. *When all else is dark, spotlights simulate moonlight, the illusion heightened by the sharp contrast of dried magnolia branches painted black and glycerinized canna leaves with luminous stark-white calla lilies.* [SUTER]

schedule with Mrs. Charles M. Fitz-Patrick, I suggested coordinating arrangements with an art-school curriculum since the Maryland Institute College of Art had been chosen as the exhibit hall. The Theme, "Fundamentals of Photography," was made-to-order for a light class if we could silhouette arrangements so as to create the effect of a photographic negative. Behind a screen, characteristics of color and texture would be obscured, and if forms were massed, they would not be defined. Therefore, we featured patterns of light and shadow rather than plant materials, and stressed the interplay of solids and spaces.

By experimenting, Mrs. Fitz-Patrick devised a method for individual display. She glued heavy tracing paper to a frame, and clamped the frame to one end of a folding aluminum table, 6 feet long by 30 inches wide. This end projected into the room; the other end was pushed against the wall. There were five tables in all, separated by aisles. This left the sides of the exhibits exposed so curious spectators, after viewing silhouettes from the front, could walk behind each screen to see how the lighting apparatus and the arrangement had been constructed.

To provide the light, a goose-neck desk lamp with a 100-watt bulb was placed on each table at the end near the wall. The arrangements were set directly behind the screen and facing it. By borrowing lamps, we avoided the cost of expensive spotlights, and the adjustable lamps permitted each contestant to illuminate her design to best effect, while directing the beam away from the line of vision. The curved reflector shades confined the light within the screen area; a spot or floodlight might have exceeded boundaries.

This system reduced problems to a minimum, but lighting can pose difficulties in flower shows if equipment is expensive and the number of outlets insufficient or inaccessible for the number of exhibits or their locations. If these obstacles can be overcome, even a few lighted arrangements greatly increase the appeal of a show.

Creating Various Effects

There are at least three ways of creating the effect of light. The first employs *actual* light to modify color. The second manipulates color to produce the *sensation* of light without special lighting. The third utilizes light-reflecting materials to increase the awareness of light, though illuminating devices need not be incorporated. You can enliven the color of textiles, objects, and flowers by coordinating them with colored incandescent lamps. Amber illumination on dull gold or copper makes these metals glow with an antique patina, and green light gives radiance to glossy, mahogany-stained weathered wood. Battery-operated flashlights (the kind sold in hardware stores but not for cameras), projected on a white arrangement of fresh materials shower it with moonbeams.

In a technique devised by Faber Birren, iridescence is created by beaming pink light on a pink design against a medium-gray background. Unusual effects result when dried flowers and foliage are painted with fluorescent paint and exposed to black light; ultraviolet rays turn white plastic purple. However, fluorescence cannot be detected except in darkness. The arrangement in color, plate 31, was photographed in a blacked-out room with four fluorescent black light tubes, 15 watts each, the sole source of light. The time exposure for the picture was about twelve seconds. The rest of the photographs in this chapter employed only the colored or white spotlights that produced the artistic effect; room lights were turned off and shades drawn to block out daylight. Generally, it increases appeal to highlight or vary color with light, but to change one hue for another arbitrarily, as one lecturer demonstrated when she converted a pale green floral design to red by means of red lamps, seems pointless and abuses the privilege light offers.

Approximating effects of light through color of plant materials is a matter of designing with color alone, and hardly pertains to lighting. It is mentioned here because the elements of color and light are interrelated and interdependent. Impressionist painters Edouard Manet and Claude Monet used dabs of color to suggest the flickering presence of light; Post-Impressionist Georges Seurat devised the pointillist technique of covering a canvas with dots of pure color that appeared luminous when viewed from a distance. To make color simulate light and produce a sunny look, instead of projecting amber and red light on an arrangement, you can get a comparable effect by the more difficult method of grading yellow and orange flowers in a pale to bright sequence. The viewer wouldn't actually see sunlight, but would experience the sensation of it.

The art of manipulating color to produce various effects of light, as luminosity, iridescence, luster, and color mist has been documented by Faber Birren in *Creative Color* and *Color, Form and Space* (both published by Reinhold Publishing Co., 1961). Since his methods can be applied to flower arrangements, these books are recommended to those interested in advanced color concepts.

Manufactured materials with high reflecting or metallic surfaces, whether seen under ordinary illumination or intensified by special lamps, offer other possibilities. But if spotlights are used, they may produce "hot spots" or glare. For this reason, on bright finishes, keep to diffused or floodlights as these generally cause fewer problems and achieve better results. Some materials you might enjoy experimenting with include colored or stained glass (lighted from behind), aluminum, chromium, copper tubing, pipes or sheets molded into forms; lamé or Lurex fabrics; and plastics. Although gilded wood is often antiqued to reduce shine and suggest age in traditional designs, bright gold imparts the quality of newness in modern arrangements.

Mirrors can produce striking effects, though small broken pieces make better designs than large sections. I like the flexible mirrored mats that disperse light; the multiple mirrored squares are glued to a mesh backing, and the mats can be rolled into a cylinder or cut into geometric shapes and sizes and cemented to a background, as shown in color plate 33. These mats are sometimes sold as table mats, but more often found in commercial displays.

Some natural materials, as jet, mica, mother-of-pearl, peacock feathers, and honesty or money-plant have an opalescent quality. Even water has a reflecting surface. Actually, iridescence is not due to pigments or dyes but to minute refractions of light that shift colors when these are seen at various angles. Intensity increases or diminishes iridescence, depending on adjacent colors. Thus pink snapdragons heighten the brilliance of peacock feathers but pale lavender Fuji chrysanthemums make them look lifeless. Some minerals have a jewel-like light, especially those covered with tiny crystals or impurities that fluoresce under black light, as the intense green Willemite from Franklin, New Jersey, the pink Calcite from Terlinqua, Texas, and the bright orange Sodalite from Moulton-boro, New Hampshire. As accessories in arrangements, these minerals are certain to attract interest.

Factors Controlling Light

You can find out about illuminating techniques as they are employed in art, interior decoration, landscaping, photography, signals, and the theater, adapting methods that are applicable or devising new ones. To achieve exactly the effects you want, you have to experiment. The behavior of light depends on so many variables, not the least are the color and texture of the objects and background it shines on, so the lighting equipment must be coordinated with the other components of a design. Here are some guidelines:

Glossy surfaces have a strong reflecting quality that produces highlights or bright patches and intensifies chroma. Light cast on such smooth textures as silk and laminates creates a sheen.

Matte finishes diffuse light; thick textures, as velvet and deep-pile materials, absorb light, causing shadows, darkening colors and generally adding richness; rough surfaces gray colors and absorb light as do dark colors.

Reds become bluer against dark backgrounds; pastels and white have a strong light-reflecting quality.

High levels of light are cheerful and stimulating; low levels, restful, and these produce an intimate atmosphere.

Diffused light reduces shadows; hard or harsh light adds sparkle to high-luster finishes, sharpens outline and form, and emphasizes contrast between lighted and unlighted areas.

For accent, illuminate from above or below with soft, tinted, and reflected light, use floodlights to "wash" over a large area.

For depth, light from more than one direction; to avoid shadows, light from both sides and "bounce" light from the ceiling.

FACTORS DETERMINING EFFECTS

Candle power: 100 watt, 150 watt incandescent; one bulb or several.

Character of light; white or chromatic—amber, blue, blue-white, green, pink, red, yellow; produced by bulbs, gelatins, cellophane or filters—warm or cool, ultraviolet or black, flashing or blinking, one color or a combination.

Direction or angle of projection: from above, behind, or below, at the side or angled; crosslighting or lighting behind transparent or translucent material, or a combination of these.

Distance between light source and arrangement.

Distribution: concentrated or diffuse, hard or soft light. Light from a one-point source as a spotlight in total darkness produces hard light, strong contrast of light and shadow. Soft light results from diffusing or spreading light at a wide angle over a large field, as from a floodlight or filtered light.

Quantity or intensity: high or low level of light, bright or dim.

In working for a special effect, you may also devise ways of illuminating arrangements in your home in the same way that you do paintings.

20
COMPETE TO WIN

You can have fun—and success—in flower-show competitions if you know how to prepare for them. Although you may feel like a rabbit running after a carrot that is always beyond reach in your pursuit of a blue ribbon, actually you may be better off not winning the first few times you exhibit. Beginner's luck is no assurance that it will continue. It may even boomerang. Exhibitors who receive a top award in their first show sometimes become so afraid of failure the next time that they are never heard from again.

This does not mean that you should not make every effort to win from the start. But if you don't, you shouldn't be discouraged. Each show you enter brings experience that pays off later. Once you acquire the knack, ribbons should come with regularity—even if they are not always blue. In fact, although you may already be seasoned, competing regularly keeps you in practice provided you enter diversified classes. Suppose you have had a winning combination with shades of purple flowers in a mass composition. Chances are that after repetition, both you and the arrangement will grow stale. Changing your designs stimulates creativity and gives your work vitality. Although fresh ideas are especially important for a new look in modern work, they also help you keep abreast of traditional styles, for these change too. The mass of yesterday was stiff, tightly packed, choked for air. Today under contemporary influences, notably the introduction of space, mass arrangements are less compact, more graceful. Innovations are contagious, one style affecting others. Practicing many trends prevents your work from being dated.

The Schedule   But regardless of how good your design or your construction, or how original your idea, few judges will be swayed if you have failed to follow the schedule. More ribbons are lost on this account than any other. The schedule details procedure; it is, therefore, called "the law of the show." And law it is with good cause. It establishes uniform requirements for all contestants and so equalizes chances of winning (like a golf handicap); at the same time it offers a common denominator for judging. Thus the test of excellence is not simply your ability to arrange, though skill in technique and design is important in evaluation. What really counts is competence, discipline, and imagination in producing a composition of high calibre that communicates a theme but observes standards of design, conforms to rules limiting choice, yet surmounts these obstacles to present a fresh concept. A tall order but nonetheless provocative. There have been not a few instances when the best arrangement in a class failed to receive even an honorable mention because it did not conform to schedule, whereas one that was hardly outstanding got the blue ribbon because it obeyed the rules.

You may be able to make a beautiful Flemish arrangement for the grand piano in your large living room, flowers spilling gracefully over the vase, but are you also able to achieve a well-proportioned effect in a niche where materials must be confined so they do not touch walls, protrude beyond the front, rest on the table, or overreach the top? Or suppose you have earned fame for your bold modern designs. Can you still produce a dramatic avant-garde composition if you are restricted to naturally dried materials in mellow tones and are forbidden the crutch of bright colors? Is your ability to arrange a pair of containers equal to your prowess with one?

There are many pitfalls in exhibiting, but you can avoid most of them by planning an arrangement that follows the wording of the schedule. Serving a double purpose, a schedule guides contestants in preparing entries; at the same time it makes clear to judges and viewers just what the exhibitor is trying to achieve. Since full details are provided on subject matter, character, number, size, and methods of staging exhibits, it is possible to form an impression of a show just by reading the schedule. However, if you have trouble understanding any of the information because, for example, the theme of the class you want to enter reads like a riddle in classical mythology, or specifications of design are vague (as unfortunately is sometimes the case), request clarification from your class consultant or the general chairman of the show. And don't permit complicated objectives to dampen your enthusiasm. More than one housewife has found fame if not fortune treading the roads to flower shows. (Yours truly, exhibit No. 1 in this case.)

Almost without exception, each flower show is based on a central theme supported by sub-themes in individual classes. Themes run the gamut of human experience; they are drawn from social and political issues, from industry, business, literature, and art, or they pertain to everyday occurrences as holidays or certain events. Although, in general, arrangements must reflect the characteristics of the overall topic, in particular, they must fulfill the specific requirements of a class. For instance, if the theme of the show were "Exploring Space," a composition of massed fruits and vegetables in an alabaster compote would be unsuitable even if the class entered were "Dining on the Moon." On the other hand, an arrangement might clearly express the character of a show but strike out on the kind of material or the container for the class. Such would be the case in an interpretation of "Country Life," that properly consisted of field flowers and roadside weeds, but lost when these were incongruously displayed in Sèvres porcelain that was too formal and grand for both title and plant material.

After stating the theme, which usually gives clues to mood, style, and perhaps color, a class may require a particular form of design, as mass, asymmetrical, abstract, etc., and indicate what it should represent as motion, tranquillity, etc. The category of plant materials may also be designated—fresh, dried, or a combination—with mention of accessories if these are permitted. Measurements and type of staging—pedestals, niches, backgrounds—determine the size, direction, and often the shape of an arrangement, whether enclosed or free-standing. Since the height of the tabletop or other surface from which it will be viewed at the show affects the perspective of a design, you should construct it at home at the same distance from the floor. This is most important.

Format of a
Schedule

A proper schedule, as proposed by the National Council of State Garden Clubs, consist of four divisions:

General Information gives the theme, date, time, and location of the show, also the names of the sponsoring group and of the committee chairmen.

Awards and Rules lists the ribbons offered with qualifications and eligibility for winning them; procedure, conditions, and responsibilities for submitting entries are stated though often separately under horticulture and artistic sections in addition to the general requirements for the show.

Horticulture and Artistic Classes, the two major competitive divisions, describes the content of the exhibits.

Advised Sections include Educational, Commercial, and Invitational displays, as well as competitive classes for children. *None of these is mandatory, unless a club is applying for a State or National Award for the entire show. Then at least two Educational Exhibits are compulsory.* Somewhat like information booths, Educational Exhibits provide literature and illustrations that teach skills pertaining to plants or promote projects connected with garden clubs. Education Exhibits are assessed, not in relation to each other, but against a perfect score of one hundred. In evaluating them, judges query: Is the information clear and adequately covered? Is staging attractive, original, appropriate? Does the Exhibit communicate? Extra credit is given for relevance to theme.

Awards   Shows accredited by National Council, *Standard Flower Shows* (the title always capitalized), must include at least five classes in horticulture and five in the artistic design division. There may be more of each, but if disproportionate, the number weighs in favor of horticulture. National Council follows the *Standard System of Awards,* which permits only one first (blue), one second (red), and one third (yellow) ribbon in each class. These awards must score respectively no less than 90, 85, and 75. At the discretion of the judges, more than one honorable mention (white) may be given.

For exceptional performance by blue-ribbon winners rated 95 or above in special categories, National Council has designated four top ribbons. Any member group, as a garden club, district or state federation can offer any or all of these provided the show qualifies in number of classes and entries and the exhibitors observe restrictions in plant materials. Since requirements differ according to awards, each specializing in one area, as natural and man-made materials, the schedule specifies what ribbons are available to contestants and what classes are eligible for each ribbon. No class or entry can ever qualify for more than one award. Generally, the top awards are differentiated by the materials of a design, as all fresh, all dried, or a choice of combinations with other objects. However, in one respect, awards are all alike; to merit any of them, an exhibit must receive a top grade in Originality and Distinction as listed in the Scale of Points.

Tricolor. Fresh plant material only.

Award of Distinction. Limited to dried materials (dehydrated by hanging, burying, or pressing), possibly combined with those that have been glycerinized or painted (designated separately as treated).

Creativity. Includes both fresh and dried, or either one, usually with a fine accessory, significant in size and importance but not dominating.

Nature, Art, and Industry (N.A.I.). Combinations of plant and man-made materials, as metals, plastics, and discards (junk).

As the need arises, National Council changes requirements for top honors, particularly in regard to accessories (which at the time of this writing are allowed for *Tricolor* and *Award of Distinction*). You should check the latest information and follow the procedures set forth in *The Handbook for Flower Shows,* published by National Council of State Garden Club, Inc., revised edition 1970), *but be guided especially by the schedule of the show you are entering.* (National Council always emphasizes this.)

Themes

Themes are broadly classified as *Decorative* or *Interpretive* and arrangements are also so designated. Although all designs are ornamental to a degree, *Decorative* ones have no other than an aesthetic purpose. Appealing to the senses, they are enjoyed purely for their harmony of form, texture, and color. However, to tie in with the topic of a particular class—a foreign country, special occasion, season, interior setting, or period in art—a composition might be obliged to stress some related characteristics, as a hot climate or a gay mood; or it could also be simply a study in contrasts, movement of line, or interplay of forms, as in the themes, "Expressway" or "Liberal Versus Conservative" or "Youth and Age."

Interpretive Designs can be Objective or Subjective. *Objective Designs* have a narrative quality. Subjects may be identified through an accessory that carries the burden of communication. Sometimes Decorative and Objective interpretations overlap, especially in traditional styles. For example, "In Black and White" a mass arrangement of fresh and dried materials would be strictly decorative since no experience is related, no object represented. But "Childhood

Reminiscences" would be Objective Interpretive since it would depend on accessories, as a rag doll or book of fairy tales to convey the idea. However, here the blend of pleasing colors and flowing lines could create such strong eye appeal that it would be Decorative as well.

An *Objective Interpretive Design* might suggest an object or experience through the design itself, its construction or color scheme, rather than through a representational figure. Such designs require a title; if they are well done, the relation between title and design is evident.

We are now considering designs of images and experiences. For example, an arrangement of zigzagging materials in shades of yellow and emanating from a light source as container would effectively interpret the theme, "Electricity." Once the shape and color of the design associates with the title, the subject is obvious. An exhibit of discarded and new materials, together with fresh and dried foliage, might leave the spectator guessing but if it were given some such caption as "Urban Renewal" the interpretation would be apparent.

Sometimes a theme can be expressed either way depending on the wording of the schedule. If the class, "Out of the Past," called for an *authentic* Neoclassical arrangement, the design would be Decorative; if for *characteristics suggesting* the Neoclassical period, the design would be an Objective Interpretation.

Subjective Interpretations, concerned with emotional response and abstract concepts, are the most provocative. They relate to what we feel and think rather than what we see. Plant materials express themes through the placement and character of lines, the interaction of forms, the relationships of colors. With few if any ties to persons, places, or things, a subjective design requires the viewer to react—positively or negatively—to draw conclusions according to his own experience. "Forecast for Tomorrow" might coordinate raw

Out of the Past. *In a class designating an* interpretation *of the same theme, this design is characteristic of the period but does not exactly conform to the style.* [KLENDER]

"NUDE DESCENDING A STAIRCASE." *A form of weathered wood appears to twist and turn like the figure in the famous, trend-setting painting by Marcel Duchamp, which provided inspiration and title for this design.* [KLENDER]

materials (plastics, metals, woods) with exotic plants in an avant-garde pattern; "Nude Descending a Staircase" (inspired by Marcel Duchamp's painting), might combine driftwood and fresh flowers in a contorted design; "Harmony Versus Cacophony" would rely on color to unify conflicting patterns of natural and man-made products. Although Subjective arrangements are more stimulating than Decorative ones, they must, nevertheless, have aesthetic value to win in a flower show.

Themes for Table Settings   Although table settings have already been discussed in Chapter 15, they are mentioned here, since like other classes in flower shows, they must interpret a theme. This can be puzzling, especially to new exhibitors who wonder how china and glassware can impart

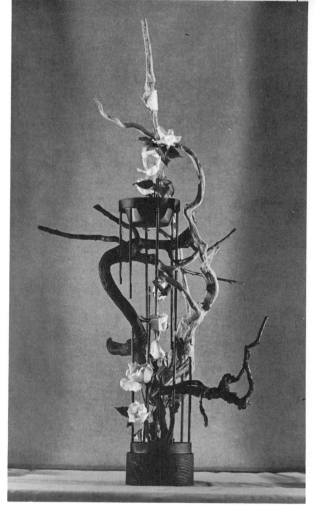

PRISON BREAK. *Illustrating "Creativity," this arrangement incorporates a pair of wrought-iron candlesticks (one inverted and both stripped of candle-holders) to make a cell from which some "inmates" escape.* [KLENDER]

ideas. Actually they don't. Aside from obvious associations of mood through color and degree of formality, appointments by themselves rarely have content, unless they happen to be decorated, as when a hunting scene is pictured. Therefore, in terms of subject matter, tableware and linen function primarily in a supporting capacity, their contribution an indication of the general character or overall tone of the theme with which they *must* be consistent. Actually the burden of communication falls on the centerpiece, and in many instances, on an accessory.

We are now back to our analysis of Decorative and Interpretive, Objective and Subjective arrangements. Thus a table setting may be a simple matter of suggesting the atmosphere for, say, a "Family

Style" buffet supper for six ("Family Style" being the theme), or the class may require a more complex interpretation like "Expectation" that would involve associations different for each contestant. To one the theme might suggest a "heavy date"; to another, a baby shower; to a third, building a new house. Although each table would create a different effect, they would all have achieved it by the same means; the appointments establishing a general tenor through the type of tableware and the color coordination, while the centerpiece told the story (though practically, an accompanying card stating the subject would be helpful). Thus though the overall effect of a table setting is usually Decorative, the arrangement itself could be an Objective or a Subjective interpretation, or it could be purely Decorative.

Here are some appropriate titles for table classes: "Drama Critic" (within an overall theme, "The Columnist"), an after-theater supper, the arrangement of dried materials and an accessory to suggest black comedy. "In the Mood," an intimate dinner for two, fresh materials only. "Pride," a Formal dinner with antique appointments (the arrangement probably tall and imposing).

Styles of Arrangements

Although the nature of the theme is designated by the schedule, the style for expressing it is usually left open, the exhibitor choosing her own. Arrangements are based on four general categories of styles:

Traditional. European period and conventional Western designs of line, mass, or massed-line.

Oriental. Heaven-man-earth compositions, usually Moribana or Nagiere.

Naturalistic. Out-of-doors representation.

Modern. Inspired by contemporary art, as abstract, or a mobile, or collage, etc.

Thus it is possible to carry out flower-show themes in various ways. An arrangement might be a Subjective Interpretation executed in modern abstract style, or it might be a Decorative Traditional Georgian composition suited to a setting in an English country estate. By encompassing all aspects of artistic design, flower shows appeal to all tastes, and at the same time keep up-to-date.

Staging   The purpose of special staging is to create an attractive setting for artistic displays, and at the same time to establish boundaries, separating one design from another. The dimensions of the space control the size of the arrangement, influencing direction and shape as well. If the area is tall and narrow, you cannot make a low horizontal design. Always compose so as to leave a comfortable margin between arrangement and staging. There should be no contact. Dimensions of the exhibition space guide proportion, the arrangement measuring no more than seven-eighths the height and three-quarters the width of the space, but not much shorter or wider than this allowance. A design that crowds the area is as much in error as one that looks lost. In turn, the size of the arrangement controls the scale of each piece of material; this should be neither too small nor too large in relation to the whole, and no one flower should be more than one-third the size of the entire arrangement. For example, if a niche is 32 inches high and the arrangement 28 inches, a 10-inch sunflower would exceed its share of space.

Since methods of staging differ, the size and shape of arrangements must be adjusted to fit each setting. The advantages of different stagings are twofold. Diversity enhances the appearance of a show and lets exhibitors experiment with various designs. The simplest staging, and the easiest for contestants, employs one or more plain walls as background for a row of entries on long tables, these covered and draped to the floor with burlap or comparable material.

Tables are marked into equal sections for each exhibit; dimensions and table height are noted in the schedule. If the background height is unlimited, an arrangement may be as tall or as short as the exhibitor wishes, provided it fits the allotted space. In this instance, contestants are generally not required to supply any other background, though they are allowed their own mat or base under the arrangement. Such staging is homelike and popular for a novice or for an "open class" in which non-members or the public may enter. This staging adapts to both simple and large-scale constructions so that no matter what the experience of the contestants, all exhibits can be accommodated.

Niches For some years, niches have been favored. Standing side by side on long tables, these cubicles, each composed of a back and two side panels, set off and partition arrangements. To estimate the proportion of arrangement to niche, select a tall container about one-third the height of the space; choose a low container of sufficient width or visual weight to be in proportion to the design whose height must still be measured in relation to the niche.

Usually, you will be required to cover only the back of the niche with material coordinated with your arrangement. Sometimes a schedule indicates that niches in one class will be painted alike by the committee to emphasize a theme. In a class "Still-Life," six mass arrangements might be displayed in niches, all covered with a rough beige fabric suggesting an artist's canvas, the floral designs then appearing as paintings. If a background is not mandatory but is allowed, it is always better to supply your own. In constant use, niches usually show signs of wear that detract from neatness; of neutral color, they rarely contribute to an exhibit. Since the purpose of a background is to set off flowers and foliage, its color, texture, and pattern can make the difference between a winner and a loser.

Yard goods is easier to attach to a niche than a rigid backing of cardboard or plywood that must be cut and finished at home. Too often when brought to the show it does not fit. It may measure exactly to the dimension in the schedule, but niches can vary a fraction of an inch and so make exact alignment impossible. Fabric, longer and wider than the back wall, can be neatly folded under at the bottom and sides of a niche and easily flung over the top to hang down behind. If yardage is ample, material need not even be taped in back as its own weight will hold it in place. And such a covering avoids the need to hem raw edges.

The sides of a niche are usually left bare (judges pretend not to notice them). However, since the tabletop on which the niche stands also serves as its floor, many exhibitors prefer to extend the background fabric to the front edge, thus concealing a table cover that may be inappropriate while creating a uniform appearance. You can experiment with wallpaper and other paper products, but they are more difficult to control.

To estimate yardage: for length, add the height and depth measurements given in the schedule plus enough extra to overlap behind and double under in front. Also allow sufficient width for turning under on each side.

Although there are no rules for draping a niche, most judges agree that a background should remain in the background. Consequently, a smooth surface is usually better than pleats or gathers. The large floral patterns of materials used for slipcovers and draperies or fabrics peppered with tiny flowers or other shapes interfere with design when they cover the area behind an arrangement. An exception might be made if the exhibit were required to coordinate materials to suggest a room setting; there, the drapery would be drawn to one side, leaving a plain area behind the floral design. A skillful arranger can sometimes use plaids and stripes to advantage if they suit the theme; thus bold contemporary patterns can be studied for effect with avant-garde constructions. As a rule, colors and textures should be of the same character as the composition. Subdued backgrounds or fine fabrics are safer with traditional and elegant subjects; bright hues and shiny surfaces often enhance modern compositions.

Backgrounds must be without crease, wrinkle, watermark, stain, or fading. Storing and transporting fabrics on rollers (never fold them to bring to a show), avoids frequent pressing. If you plan to exhibit regularly, build up a supply of backgrounds to go with your containers and accessories. At remnant counters, dress and drapery materials are often sold for a fraction of their value. But check carefully for adequate size.

Since niches are not available commercially, their specifications vary according to the needs of the group constructing them. The dimensions used by a small club may be quite different from those of a state federation or plant society. Sometimes a club changes an obsolete size when replacing worn-out models. Therefore, each time you enter a show, check the measurements. If your club is in the market for new niches, the size recommended by the National Council is 40 inches high, 32 inches wide, and 18 inches deep.

Bases in Niches The proportion of an arrangement to a niche is important in judging. On this account the use of a base should be decided in the initial planning so as to allow for its thickness in the overall measurement of the design. Never add a base as an afterthought unless you are certain that it does not raise the arrangement above the margin at the top of the niche.

If a base is necessary, compensate for its height by choosing a shorter container. For example, in a 40-inch niche, the height of a container would be about 13 inches. However, if a 2-inch base were used, the space would not accommodate a container more than 11 inches tall. In reverse, if you had just the right vase, but it was only 10 inches high, placing it on a 3-inch platform would increase height to the proper proportion. Since in this instance it would serve a practical purpose, the base would not necessarily be visible. If you lacked an appropriate decorative one, you could elevate the design on a wooden block or box and conceal this under the background fabric that also covers the floor of the niche.

Backboards   Colored poster boards are beginning to replace niches. They are especially suitable for modern compositions since the absence of side panels allows greater freedom of design. Show requirements for backboards vary. Sometimes all are assigned in a uniform hue; sometimes exhibitors may choose from an assortment of colors. In most cases, a base is permitted, but as always, it should make a definite contribution to the overall effect and allowance made for it at the outset.

Pedestals   Most flower shows offer one or more pedestal classes. Pedestals may stand in an open area or be staged against a wall. Although generally no other background is required, it is customary for exhibitors to cover the pedestal top (which may be square, round, or rectangular) with a mat of paper cut to fit, a fabric lying on top (edges tucked under), material spread tablecloth fashion with a short drop, or fabric stretched over the top and tacked underneath. Although there is no fixed ratio of arrangement to pedestal, a design should look comfortable on its perch. Since some judges allow plant materials to extend below the pedestal top, and others rule against it, check show policy before constructing an arrangement or play safe and keep it within bounds.

One point often overlooked is the height of a pedestal. Composing at a different level from the one for display changes perspective, perhaps to the extent of ruining an arrangement. If you practice the design on a table at home, and then stand it on a taller pedestal at a show, the elevation may expose more of the lower part than the face. Thus changing point-of-view as little as 3 to 4 inches can be disastrous. As a test, move to the mantle an arrangement you are accustomed to see at eye-level. The distortion will make such an impression that you are unlikely thereafter to disregard exhibition height from the floor when you make your arrangement at home.

Platforms Platforms make effective staging for modern designs. Similar to a collapsed card table (which is often used), and resting directly on the floor, one platform assigned each exhibitor in a class makes possible the display of compositions 4 to 6 feet high. These may be free-standing or shown against a wall. In the same category are low tables appropriate for Japanese-type arrangements made "to be viewed from above," as the schedule is likely to phrase it. Sometimes water-reflecting compositions are constructed horizontally, the top surface slightly concave. The viewer looks down into the design, rather than seeing it head-on. Again, since the low level is important to the perspective, rehearse the arrangement at home in a mock-up of the show setting.

I can remember making one of these Oriental platform arrangements some years ago. Working at a higher level than the one directed by the schedule, I constructed an upright frontal design; it was wrong for the class and earned me only disappointment. In large vertical arrangements, the schedule often guides proportion and scale by designating height. A given height might require adjusting the center of interest. Other dimensions would be determined by the size of the platform.

Vignettes The term vignette refers to an exhibit incorporating furniture of standard size with an arrangement to represent the character of an entire room. The staging, creating an effect like that of a niche, may consist of a full-sized screen, as enclosure. A carpet, drapery, pictures, and other accessories may be included. These are furnished by the exhibitor as part of the design and *not* by the staging committee. The furnishings establish the style, period, or occasion of the setting, which may constitute the theme of the class or relate to it. Since this is really an exercise in interior decorating, all components must be correlated. Harmony and pictorial quality together receive major consideration in judging.

The choice of furniture depends on the dimensions of the space, and that in turn determines proportion and scale. Since the area, even though life-size, is often not very large due to the space limitations of a show, scatter rugs, and small chairs, tables, or chests are preferred to massive pieces. The greater their size, the less the number that can be accommodated. The arrangement must take its normal place in relation to the setting. Therefore, the furniture that holds it controls the proportion and scale of the floral design rather than the dimensions of staging as would be the case when an arrangement is shown by itself against its own background. Thus, a cigarette table would require a smaller arrangement than a wide chest, even though this too might be small. A multifaceted problem, a vignette necessitates considerable thought, planning, and physical effort, but worth the hardships in charm.

Shadow Boxes   Shadow boxes have long been an aspect of flower shows, but since they rely primarily on lighting for effect, they are difficult for the exhibitor to execute and the committee to stage. Consequently, shadow boxes are more usual in large shows and there they make a dramatic contribution. In a shadow box, an arrangement stands behind a framed sheetlike screen and only the silhouette, projected by a rear light, is seen. Since interior details are obscured, plant materials merge into a solid mass unless separated by spaces within the composition that are essential to it.

A unique aspect of shadow box designs is the diminished importance of texture since it is no longer readily discernible; color now functions, not as a schemed harmony but as gradation and contrast between light and dark areas. The effect is similar to that of a black-and-white photograph where interplay of positive and negative relationships are emphasized. Condition of material is also minimized, since defects unless blatant are unlikely to show. Proportion and scale remain paramount, with line, shape, and pattern of design having the greatest influence on the judging.

Judging   It helps to know how exhibits are evaluated; then you can guard against mistakes when preparing for a show. Contrary to popular opinion, judges do not compare one entry with another. Instead, each is rated against perfection (rarely achieved), merits are rewarded and faults penalized according to a Scale of Points that totals one hundred.

Points are not the same for all shows; indeed, they may vary among classes. In large shows, it is not uncommon to find the Scale of Points that will be used given in the schedule. In small shows this seldom occurs. However, most judging takes place informally on the basis of general considerations relevant to nearly all exhibits. No matter what the style of arrangement, judges are concerned primarily with conformance to schedule or interpretation of theme, competence of design, handling of color, condition of materials (damaged or wilted), originality of concept, and distinction in execution. In a close contest, each category receives a numerical evaluation to help in determining the winner. Thus, out of a possible score of 40 for Design, an exhibit may rate only 35, perhaps because the balance tips slightly forward or dominance is inadequate. If Originality and Distinction together are worth 20 points, full credit might be given if the composition were unusually creative and well constructed.

Although Conformance to Schedule does not always appear as a separate category in a Scale of Points, nevertheless, observance of rules and class requirements must be established before an entry can be evaluated in other respects. Failure to comply results in disqualification by the Classification Chairman whose duty it is to check violations before judging. If judges detect errors overlooked, they deduct enough points from an offending arrangement to eliminate chances for a high award. Conformance can be so tricky that an exhibitor may err without realizing. Here are some examples: In a class designating *fresh garden* materials, florist roses and dried wisteria curls would not be permitted. (Note here, too, that in a display of bare branches in a *fresh* class, a green leaf or bud should be visible as evidence the material is alive.) When only *naturally* dried flowers and foliage are called for, don't paint or shellac even one leaf unless the schedule allows it. If competing in a *period* class, don't enter a Japanese arrangement; this is considered a style. To interpret "A Popular Song" in an overall theme, "Trends of *Today*," stay away from old favorites. In a class designating *free-form* design, beware of a geometric container. For "An *Impromptu* Seated Dinner," judges will not look favorably on an arrangement of costly flowers.

Other obvious errors might include the use of an accessory where none was allowed; fresh plant materials in a dried class; an asymmetrical composition if the theme called for formal symmetry; a contemporary arrangement in a schedule for abstract; failure to feature characteristics intended to predominate or to symbolize the theme; improper construction, as a design completed only in front although it is to be free-standing and seen from all sides.

Conservation Material Each garden federation of National Council has a designated group of native plants (especially wild flowers) that are in danger of extinction. To protect these plants, each state compiles its own Conservation List of materials forbidden to exhibitors. It matters not if a contestant grows them in her own garden, the interdict remains. However, *restrictions only apply to materials listed by the state in which the show is held, not to other states where some plants may be hardier and so safer.* Desert spoons are on the Conservation List in Arizona, but may be used in Maryland where they do not grow. Rhododendron is forbidden in New York, but not in Maryland, so I would be allowed to display it in my state but not in a New York show.

Most judges are familiar with the protected plants in their states and instantly recognize them in a show. Should an entry include even one tiny forbidden flower, the offending exhibit is treated as though it had leprosy and is categorically eliminated. Conservation

Lists are usually available through state federation offices. Since changes are occasionally made, competitors should get these lists and refer to them when in doubt. If you give lecture-demonstrations and inadvertently include in your program conservation material of the state your are visiting, you will have committed a serious faux pax. (I know, I once was guilty.)

Theme Interpretation

To interpret a theme correctly, plant materials should have characteristics related to the idea they are supposed to convey. If they are unsuitable, the character or tone of the composition will not be right. Therefore, consider associations between moods and forms, colors, and textures, since one flower is likely to communicate a particular idea better than another. For example, gladioli express line, but not rhythm. Lilies suggest reverence; daisies, gaiety. The texture of yarrow is more informal than that of a rose. Red carnations make a brighter palette than pink ones.

Plant origins are another influence. Creating the proper historical, geographic, or seasonal atmosphere depends on availability of materials to a particular situation. For instance, ginger would be out of context in a William and Mary period piece; daffodils do not represent the tropics, nor chrysanthemums, spring.

Originality and Distinction

The two qualities judges seek most in arrangements are Originality and Distinction. They appear with regularity on Scales of Points, for without them no exhibit can win a top award. Yet to many contestants, the riddle of what constitutes Originality and Distinction remains unsolved. Somehow it is easier to describe examples than to give definitions. In a sense, the effect of Originality and Distinction is akin to that of a good billboard advertisement that captures attention, holds interest long enough to convey a message, and, at the same time, evokes a favorable response. A design must be different, contain an element of surprise, an individual touch if it is to give evidence of Originality and Distinction. It can even be unorthodox, but not so far out as to be unrecognizable by current standards, and never bizarre.

To judges, Originality and Distinction imply a fresh approach manifested in any of several ways: the use of common materials in a new guise; an old theme with a novel twist; innovative design; interesting spatial relationships perhaps adding further dimension to design; adept handling of unusual color combinations; mastery of difficult construction or of materials known to be contrary; or any component as a container, plant material, or accessory that is out-of-the-ordinary. In short, they look for that special something that sets one exhibit apart from the crowd.

It is interesting to note, too, that Originality and Distinction often serve as a catch-all for deficiencies not otherwise provided for in a Scale of Points. For instance, if mechanics are exposed or faulty, they detract from Distinction and so points are deducted under that category. If foliage is droopy, a container leaks or is chipped, a base scratched, unless Condition has been listed, penalty is drawn from Distinction. On the other hand, proficiency in mechanics or freshness of difficult-to-harden materials are examples of merits rewarded here too.

Think of originality in terms of two competing exhibits. The theme is "Halloween." Entry No. 1 features a witch's hat as container for dried fall flowers and fresh autumn foliage. A suitable interpretation, but not very imaginative. Entry No. 2, striving for an eerie effect, presents a silhouette-type design of bare black branches weaving in and out of space and punctuated by bright orange chrysanthemums, a vivid contrast against a gray background. Appropriate, yes, but most of all, subtle, creative, and artistic. Although exhibitors claim that Originality and Distinction require an innate creative spark and consequently cannot be taught, I contend that they can be developed. It is a matter of being observant; of examining, studying, and experimenting with relationships of form, color, and texture for the design effects they can produce. When you see forms, analyze their potential, pick out their assets. Ask yourself, how will they combine with something else? What qualities do they lack that must be supplied from another source to produce contrast, extend line, or enlarge shape?

Train to Win   To develop your skill, visit shows and notice the comments that judges write on the exhibit cards, explaining inadequacies or suggesting improvements. It may even help you to compile a list to check your own entries for errors. Practice interpreting schedules, either mentally or in actual competition. Often schedules are available in advance, so spend time dreaming up designs even if you don't plan to enter. Then attend the show to find out how your ideas compare with those of the winners. This practice stimulates your thinking and awakens you to possibilities you may not have considered. When you do compete, always analyze your design in relation to those of others for methods of approach, new avenues of interpretation, features to emphasize or soft-pedal. Once you gain proficiency in one type of design, move on to another, perhaps of a different type, or with greater challenge. By continuing to enlarge your experience, you will improve your work.

Checklist for   In preparing an exhibit for a flower show, study the general rules
Success   carefully and keep in mind the overall theme; in addition, follow these guidelines:

MEASUREMENTS

Will size (of the exhibit) fit the space in height, width, depth, quantity (of plant materials), and visual weight?

CHARACTER

Are colors, textures, and style appropriate for the theme? Do they aid in conveying the idea, and are they compatible?

PLANT MATERIALS

Are flowers and foliage within the category designated for the class? Do they qualify for the award sought, and are they related in origin to the topic?

DESIGN

Does the form of design conform exactly to the one requested in the schedule, if specifically a line, abstract, asymmetrical, etc.?

ARTICLES

Have you included all articles required, such as a background, or the correct number of appointments for a table setting but *only* those articles permitted? Have you incorporated an accessory where none was allowed?

CONDITION

Are all components free of defects? Is plant material fresh? Has it been properly hardened?

COMPOSITION

Is balance visually stable? Are flowers and foliage neatly organized into a cohesive unit, and has the design been finished at the rear?

CONSTRUCTION

Are mechanics sufficiently sturdy? Have they been well-anchored, and are they able to hold materials firmly in place when subjected to the hazards of exhibition?

Flower-show competition is a fine outlet for a creative mind. It provides opportunity to display both your ability and your prized possessions. Best of all, it brings a sense of achievement and the recognition that many of us seek.

21

THE FLOWER ARRANGER'S GARDEN

I planted my garden to give me materials for flower arranging. My original purpose was simply to fill the yard with decorative plants to cut with no thought of their importance in the landscape. They were not expected to make a setting for my home, nor, alas, places of rest or recreation for my family, but just flowers and foliages for my special purposes.

In proper landscape design, plants are in proportion to the property, suited to growing conditions of the site, and massed in groups of one kind; tall plants make a background for shorter ones that provide transition to ground covers and lawn. Such a garden presents a pleasing picture. Mine was a perfect example of what not to do.

Although I might have bought and arranged my plants according to a landscape plan, I did not think such a planting would be sufficiently rich in quantity or variety to satisfy my desire for beautiful and unusual foliage throughout the year. What I wanted was a large collection of evergreens, each one different, to guarantee a wide choice for arrangements, especially in winter. Since fresh flowers are always available from florists, and my own cupboard bulges with dried and artificial materials, all I needed was a private garden of greens. Then, whenever I felt the urge to arrange, no matter what the season, I had only to step outside and cut.

Plants that Came
with the House

When we bought our traditional, red-brick house, it was thirty-five years old and had been vacant almost a year. Although it was in the city, the property measured nearly an acre and the grounds certainly needed refurbishing. Most of the trees and shrubs were neither unusual nor adaptable for indoor designs. A huge linden sheltered the house but in summer cast shade and debris everywhere. Beneath it lay barren ground and on slopes in front and at the side scraggly barberry prevented erosion. Surrounding the place on three sides were more giant lindens, an oak and a horse chestnut that blocked out the sun. What lawn there was was a sight.

There were various other plants, yews, a blue spruce, a hedge of overgrown azaleas that never flowered, an American holly with leaf miner, and a few pines that looked like discarded Christmas trees. A cypress and a red pine were useful for cutting and we did have a lovely pink crape myrtle, but my husband chopped it down the first winter, thinking it was dead. The one flower bed was overrun with weedy perennial phlox interspersed with a few ancient rose bushes. A hedge of peonies tried valiantly to bloom, but the shade of the big oak prevented any display. There was an apple tree with wormy fruit, a crab apple my children called the bubble-gum tree, a weeping cherry, and three vintage lilacs with only the strength to produce one flower each—a disappointment, as I am especially fond of arranging lavender lilacs with pink or red tulips.

On the plus side were a towering *Magnolia grandiflora*, a *Viburnum carlesii* with curving branches and fragrant blossoms, and a spectacular sorrel tree with scarlet foliage and pendulous clusters of tiny white flowers in fall. It stood beside a sweet-scented deciduous *Magnolia virginiana*. Indispensable for any arranger was the corky, winged euonymous *Euonymus alatus*, perfect with or without foliage for linear designs; also, three huge boxwoods useful for filler in mass compositions, and a wealth of ivy. I use the trailing tendrils to cascade from tall containers, cluster the leaves into rosettes for focal areas, or place one or two to conceal the rim of a vase and create transition from the arrangement. Though the old garden contained some useful plants, I needed many more.

Plants I Couldn't Resist

I began adding to the garden at random whenever I saw a plant with foliage that attracted me. Never more than one plant of a kind. I would cart it home, stick it anywhere I could find space, and assumed, even expected, that it would grow. I shopped nursery catalogues with the same unconcern for environmental requirements; needless to say, some of my purchases died. Ultimate size didn't deter me, for constant cutting for arrangements prevents trees and shrubs from realizing their potential.

The more I saw, the less I could resist buying. I recall that my earliest purchases included a weigela to provide pink flowers and curving branches for horizontal designs, photinia for its whorled leaf growth appropriate for centers of interest, gold-dust aucuba for its strong variegated foliage, and a camellia for its beautiful flowers and branching habits, as well as its year-round, rich green leaves.

I discovered flowering plum. It was love at first sight, and my ardor has never waned for the longer I use it, the more I value it. I can hardly wait for the leaves to open and mature in warm weather when foliage color is almost unique. It tones in with pinks and reds as well as with yellow and orange. Although plum branches do not hold up if cut while growth is new and tender, mature foliage lasts well if properly hardened beforehand by soaking branches in water. Plum is so versatile it suits both mass and linear compositions, and can also be glycerinized. If you don't have this tree and can grow it in your area (not below zero), by all means, plant it. I can't do without mine.

One of my first teachers, a *grande dame* of the art of flower arranging, introduced me to leucothoe. The table centerpieces she made with it were outstanding. To acquire one of these evergreen shrubs became my goal. Described in horticulture manuals as drooping, true to its name the slender branches send forth a shower of white flowers between pointed and colorful leaves. Resembling andromeda, with which it is sometimes confused, leucothoe, green or variegated—mine is 'Girard's Rainbow'—is most desirable in winter when the foliage turns a pleasing bronze. A must for every arranger's garden if conditions are favorable, it can also be glycerinized.

An experienced member of my garden club led me to another treasure when she brought cuttings of a trifoliate orange to one of our meetings. She told us cuttings should be rooted in water and then planted outside. Mine grew well and developed into a sturdy treelike shrub that I like to cut for modern designs. Branches pruned to a strong line or massed as a thicket always look dramatic when I exhibit them in arrangements.

In my search for plant materials, I hunted everywhere—nurseries, flower shows, arboretums, parks, and gardens (both public and private). By studying horticultural publications as well, I became familiar with plants I never knew existed, and each time a new one captivated me, I was obsessed with a desire to obtain it.

PURE LINE. *If you can brave the thorns, trifoliate orange makes an effective arrangement, green, or dried and painted; here, with clusters of variegated aucuba in a pot by Cecil Mercer.* [KLENDER]

NEEDLED AND BROAD-LEAVED. *Cherry laurel contrasts with juniper in form, texture, and color.* [KLENDER]

Space was running out. I began replacing shrubs and trees I didn't want with those I did. The barberries on the slopes were the first to go. Then in swift succession the apple was axed and some of the pine trees. I found a place to wedge in a 'Burfordii' holly to cut for holiday designs. Driving by the Walters Art Gallery, I noticed some ligustrum. Its glossy foliage appealed to me and I knew it would make a good hedge, filler for arrangements, and stakes for fastening fruits and vegetables in table designs. Deviating from my usual procedure of buying only one, I planted six. At the same time I had to discard a recently acquired vernal witch-hazel afflicted with gall. However, it was no loss as I had bought the wrong variety, and now the site was available for a Japanese flowering quince.

Still there was all that lawn, most of it weeds. If I eliminated it,

I could have the room I so desperately wanted for ornamentals, and then I would never have to bother about a lawn mower or read another article on lawn care again. I resolved that the grass must go.

Enter the Landscape Architect

If you have been counting, you are probably wondering where I managed to put all the many plants I was acquiring. Not only had I run out of space, but my inattention to design had produced such a mishmash that even I could no longer live with the mess I had made. Clearly an expert was needed to restore order, but it was essential to find someone flexible enough to agree to my unorthodox requirements. Furthermore, I needed a landscape architect to guide me in locating and identifying the many varieties I was still discovering.

Between the time of my first purchase and my decision to seek professional advice, I had become more experienced in flower arranging—exhibiting in shows, lecturing, and joining advanced study groups—and I had also earned my certificate as a National Accredited Flower Show Judge. My training in National Council flower-show schools had taught me the essentials of design. Now, instead of buying on impulse, I tried to choose plants that would contribute definite qualities to an arrangement, unusual shapes, curving or angular lines, dense or sparse form, and variations in colors, textures, and patterns of foliage. So I became convinced that my garden could not only provide me with a steady supply of materials for decorating my home and competing in shows, but it could also provide an attractive setting for the house.

A Plan for My Garden

By the time I found a sympathetic landscape architect, it was September. Although he protested at first, he agreed to make a design without a blade of grass on the entire property. To replace the lawn, he incorporated ground covers, a patio with a small pool in the corner, more trees and shrubs, and tons and tons of tanroot mulch. As he himself had no interest in garden flowers, he made no provi-

My Early Morning View. *Japanese cut-leaf red maple, set off by blue juniper, makes a lovely picture to start the day. Planting design by Kurt Bluemel.* [SUTER]

Country in the City. *A pool in the corner of the patio is alive with fish, lotus, papyrus, and water iris. Pool design by Wolfgang Oehme.* [SUTER]

sion for cutting beds, and even destroyed the one I had. This, I promised myself, would have to be remedied.

Our breakfast room opened onto the back yard. When the garden was completed, windows that had overlooked a vista of weeds, now framed a patio. An open area had been created in the center to display one of my favorites, a dwarf, cut-leaf, red Japanese maple. To set it off, a rug of creeping blue Wilton juniper was added for contrasting color and texture. This composition is so appealing that I enjoy it every morning year after year. As I watch my new plants grow, I mentally prune them for arrangements as I drink my breakfast coffee.

From this central planting my gaze now wanders to the ornamental grasses that frame the pool. In summer, water plants grow there in submerged pots—papyrus, water iris, water-lilies, and a spectacular lotus. The scene is so restful that the holly, now freed of

miner, no longer offends me and the azalea hedge at the head of the pool has begun to bloom again. The picture is completed by a pendulous deodar cedar that stretches out over the pond.

Many kinds of ground covers now furnish me with large individual leaves so necessary for accents in arrangements. Some produce flowers as well. In addition to ivy, I planted anchusa, astilbe, bergenia, daylilies, ferns, heather, hosta, ligularia, liriope, pachysandra, yucca, and for miniature floral designs, ajuga, myrtle, and sedum.

Along one side of the patio majestic old boxwoods are flanked by two small sunny plots. In one, I grow dahlias among pink loosestrife and blue veronica; in the other, my favorites, ornamental cabbage and kale with purple-berried callicarpa, a pink spiraea, echinops, liatris, and yellow tritoma.

Essential Evergreens

Shopping for new trees and shrubs for landscape effects began to fascinate me. I have always admired *Cedrus atlantica glauca* for its blue foliage (a color scarce in plants) and its gracefully curving branches, so attractive with red carnations in centerpieces for Christmas. In a nursery I found a Japanese crytomeria and the more unusual *C. japonica* 'Dacrydioides', its thin spiny branches terminating in short sprays. A *Chamaecyparis obtusa* 'Corralliformis' appealed for its strangely twisting shape and golden-green hue, as did an umbrella-pine, *Sciadopitys*. Since all were suited to the growing conditions I could provide, I had them transferred to my garden.

Junipers were another obsession for their bluish hue. In addition to the Wilton that I now had, I chose *Juniperus chinensis* 'Meyeri', 'Sargentii', *J. tamariscifolia,* and 'Waukegan' some growing upright, others spreading. We clustered these with the weeping cherry at the front edge of the property and the purple wisteria tree I had acquired some years ago.

No arranger's garden is complete without broadleaved evergreens. Three varieties of mahonia—*M. aquifolium, bealii* and *pinnata*—of different habit and leaf size and nandina were included for Japanese arrangements. For traditional designs I stocked cherry and mountain-laurel, leatherleaf viburnum, rhododendron, Russian-olive, skimmia, and the unusual *Cotoneaster salicifolia floccosa.* Different kinds of hollies seemed a necessity. I chose three cultivars of *Ilex altaclarensis*—*hodginsi, nobilis,* and *shepherdi*—also *I. pernyi* 'East Palatka', and a new introduction by Kingsville Nurseries in Maryland, Brownell special. Along with these came an osmanthus and a lovely shrub called *Stranvaesia davidiana,* which is deciduous.

When contorted plants like fantail and corkscrew willow and the tortured Harry Lauder's Walking Stick caught the fancy of arrangers, I added them to my collection. Seeing it in a flower show,

FOR CUTTING. *A back section of the garden yields umbrella pine,* Cotoneaster salicifolia flocosa, Cryptomeria japonica 'Dacrydioides,' *Japanese cryptomeria, camellia, and a groundcover of lirope.* [SUTER]

I acquired the sapphire-berry, *Symplocos paniculata* for its bright-blue fruit rare in hardy woody plants, and near it I planted the fragrant winter-hazel, valuable for its branching pattern, foliage, and clusters of yellow spring flowers.

To round out my foliage materials, I squeezed in a plant each of Scotch broom, enkianthus, clethra, pyracantha, evergreen euonymus, a pink dogwood, andromeda, bamboo, three small ivy shrubs, *Hedera arborescens,* and replacements for the ancient lilacs. I included a redbud, but since this is on the Maryland conservation list, I cannot exhibit it in shows here, perhaps a reason to give it to our garden center and replace it with something else.

Need for Flowers

Now I wanted roses of all colors, not just one shade in a landscape group. A small sunny plot beside the breakfast room was made to order, one the architect had designated for his own favorite, the devil's walking stick. I never acquired a taste for this aralia and finally gave it to my neighbor. The twelve hybrid teas bordered with geraniums and miniature boxwoods that replaced it have produced a wealth of fragrant colorful blooms for both outdoors and inside pleasure through summer and much of fall.

A cutting garden of bulbs, annuals, and perennials was, of course, essential. When I asked the architect to find room for this, he pondered briefly and then suggested I tear down the house. It occupied, he said, the only large open sunny site on the property. So far as he was concerned, the matter was closed.

But I had a really sensible idea. Along the east side of the house was a slope where the soil tended to wash, but it did receive considerable sun. Wouldn't it look attractive, I reasoned, terraced with planter boxes? The architect agreed to submit a design. It was exactly what I wanted—three tiers of redwood boxes, twenty-one units in all, seven on each level. A flagstone walk separated them into triangular sections that permitted access for maintenance. Now I could have flowers, lots of them. For a succession of spring bloom,

A DRIFT OF PERFUME. *In the garden or the house, the fragrance of* Viburnum carlesii *pervades the air; in a Japanese compote, branches appear to grow behind a clump of daffodils.* [SUTER]

the architect recommended Emperor and Triumph tulips in red, pink, gold, and white, some in all three tiers, Dutch iris, blue, yellow, and cream, each in a section on the top level, and lavender anemones in the center box. I added daffodils, the double 'Golden Orchid' and 'Von Sion', a fascinating yellow-and-green bicolor. The second year, these flowers made such a grand show that I didn't cut a single bloom for fear of spoiling the effect.

The few remaining boxes were filled with Shelford Hybrid eremurus, physostegia, and stokesia, perennials not commonly used in arrangements, and some lilies for June, July, and August—'Jamboree' (a Rubrum with wonderful fragrance), the orange 'Connecticut Yankee' and yellow 'Destiny', also several giant allium for early June color.

In August and September the boxes overflowed with annuals—celosia, marigolds, and zinnias, all long-lasting when fresh and good

SUMMER FLOWERS. *From the border, a mixed bouquet in a washed pewter compote.* [SUTER]

for drying. Later ambition drew me to such perennials as bells-of-Ireland, dusty-miller, gaillardia, and snapdragons—the seedlings tucked here and there between tulips and iris. Space beside the boxes was filled with a few yarrow plants and a spot close by provided just enough room for twelve red cannas with bronze leaves.

There was no place in the boxes for the sizable sunflowers and castor bean I wanted, so I seeded these here and there at the back of the property near some blue hydrangeas. The seedlings of ornamental basil that I bought at a plant auction were a mistake. Although the deep red foliage is attractive, basil reseeds so prolifically it can inundate even a big property. Visiting gardens and seed farms, I continued to find a new flowers of interest, especially those suited to drying, everlastings, statice, and strawflowers.

Although planting materials for flower arranging have been emphasized, I have discovered that a good landscape design can also be achieved.

INDEX